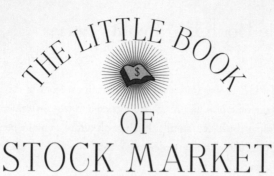

# THE LITTLE BOOK
# OF
# STOCK MARKET
# PROFITS

# Little Book Big Profits Series

In the *Little Book Big Profits* series, the brightest icons in the financial world write on topics that range from tried-and-true investment strategies to tomorrow's new trends. Each book offers a unique perspective on investing, allowing the reader to pick and choose from the very best in investment advice today.

Books in the *Little Book Big Profits* series include:

# THE LITTLE BOOK

## OF

# STOCK MARKET PROFITS

*The Best Strategies of All Time*

*Made Even Better*

## MITCH ZACKS

WILEY

John Wiley & Sons, Inc.

Published by John Wiley & Sons, Inc., Hoboken, New Jersey.
Published simultaneously in Canada.

For general information on our other products and services or for technical support, please contact our Customer Care Department within the United States at (800) 762-2974, outside the United States at (317) 572-3993 or fax (317) 572-4002.

Wiley also publishes its books in a variety of electronic formats. Some content that appears in print may not be available in electronic books. For more information about Wiley products, visit our web site at www.wiley.com.

*Library of Congress Cataloging-in-Publication Data:*

Zacks, Mitch.
    The little book of stock market profits : the best strategies of all time made even better / Mitch Zacks. — 1
    p. cm. — (Little book, big profits series)
    ISBN 978-0-470-90341-4 (hardback); 978-1-118-19241-2 (ebk); 978-1-118-19243-6 (ebk); 978-1-118-19244-3 (ebk)
    1. Stocks.   2. Investment analysis.   3. Speculation.   I. Title.
    HG4661.Z33 2011
    332.63'22—dc23

                                                                        2011033520

Printed in the United States of America

10 9 8 7 6 5 4 3 2 1

# Contents

# Introduction

As the old joke goes, the best way to make a small fortune in the stock market is to start with a large fortune. Given the volatility and sharp downturns in the market since the 2008 financial crisis, it's understandable that many investors might be wary about investing in equities these days.

With the market under intense pressure following the historic downgrade of the United States' credit rating, equity investment is not a hot topic. Many pundits argue that the malaise in the market is reflective of a declining American empire. They point overseas toward the East or bury their heads in the sand to look for shiny rocks called gold. This negative sentiment—while understandable—is actually very good news for investors. Stocks, currently, are on sale.

This is not the first time, nor the last, that stocks will likely prove to be a good investment. In fact, since World War II, the U.S. stock market has been able to generate annualized returns that are about 6 percent over the rate of return of Treasury bills.

These stock market returns occurred despite numerous obstacles. Over the past 60 years, we have witnessed the Cold War, the Cuban Missile Crisis, the Vietnam War, the Korean War, the stagflation and oil crisis of the 1970s, the Watergate scandal, double-digit interest rates, the Stock Market Crash of 1987, the dot-com crash in the early 2000s, the real estate crash, the financial implosion of 2008, as well as massive political upheavals, cultural revolutions, and manias—in the face of all these obstacles, the market marched forward. The future will bring its share of problems and I have no doubt they will be just as serious as what we have experienced in the past. But just as in the past, I am confident they will be overcome.

As always, the best way to generate returns in the equity markets is to invest and to stay invested over a long period of time. Rapid-fire day trading, in particular, is far too volatile and risky to actually generate long-term wealth.

The key to equity investing is to not become too exuberant in the periods of stock market gains and to not become too despondent when the market sells off. Levelheaded commitment to equities is what is necessary to generate real returns.

You must have the strength of mind to look past the volatility of the present and realize that if you invest over the long-term, substantial returns can be generated by holding equities.

Based on a foundation of academic research, *The Little Book of Stock Market Profits* explains how to build long-term wealth in the equity markets. The book focuses on investment strategies that will help an investor prudently navigate the market regardless of its level of volatility. Each chapter focuses on a specific means of selecting stocks that can potentially generate *alpha*, or the value that a professional investor adds to a fund's return. Alpha is the white whale of the investment business. It is what professional investors devote their careers to discovering. Quite simply, the search for alpha is a quest to find a means of selecting stocks that will generate performance greater than the level of risk borne. The search for alpha is not so much trying to find a free lunch in the equity markets, as much as it is the art of using statistics to identify groups of stocks that will beat the market.

*The Little Book of Stock Market Profits* identifies and analyzes the major methods documented by finance researchers that can be used by investors to generate alpha. My book draws upon the survey of over 650 research papers published over the past 20 years that are summarized in *The Handbook of Equity Market Anomalies* also published by John Wiley & Sons (2011). In *The Little Book of Stock Market Profits,* I synthesize, explain, and interpret the cutting-edge academic research relevant to equity investing and combine it with my own insight gained as a portfolio manager.

If implemented correctly, the information in this book could help you beat the market. Here is a breakdown of what's discussed in each chapter:

- Chapter 1 examines how best to use sell-side analyst recommendations in an investment process. The answer is counterintuitive, but nonetheless powerful.
- Chapter 2 asks whether it makes sense to tilt a portfolio toward smaller cap stocks. The results are not what conventional wisdom indicates.
- Chapter 3 explains how earnings estimates can generate alpha. I have been using earnings estimate revisions as a source of alpha for more than a decade and a half and am a firm believer in their efficacy.
- Chapter 4 looks at whether price momentum can be used to identify stocks that will outperform the market. New research indicates that if you are not entering a recession, price momentum can be a very effective tool.
- Chapter 5 is about piggybacking. We look into whether piggybacking on the trades of insiders can help increase returns. It seems reasonable that if

the CEO of a company is buying his own stock, that perhaps you should as well.

- Chapter 6 covers the signaling effects of net stock issuance activity. Hopefully, by the end of this chapter you will agree with Groucho Marx and pass on the next IPO offered to you but embrace a company engaging in a stock buy-back.

- Chapter 7 shows that excess returns may be generated by focusing on the quality of earnings a company generates. The biggest challenge is whether the results have already been arbitraged away by professional investors.

- Chapter 8 illustrates the importance of using valuation metrics in trying to find stocks with positive alpha. It appears that Graham and Dodd's insights were eerily prescient.

- Chapter 9 focuses on a phenomenon called post-earnings announcement drift and illustrates how an investor can use earnings surprises to generate returns that are higher than one would expect, given the risk being taken.

- Chapter 10 looks into whether seasonal timing strategies can beat the market. Generally, I tend to discount market-timing strategies, but the results may be very interesting to futures traders.

- Chapter 11, the last chapter, examines the creation of multi-factor models that can generate excess returns. One of the multiple-factor models works better among growth stocks, while the other is more appropriate for value investing.

By the end of this book, you will hopefully understand how various methodologies can help you beat the market. Most likely the next decade will prove to be a very good time to start implementing these strategies.

I would venture to say that, given the level of pessimism permeating the country and the markets, savvy investors entering the equity markets and holding stocks over the next decade will be nicely rewarded. Most likely, equity returns over the next 10 years will be greater than they have been over the previous 10 years, which by any measure has been a dreadful decade for equities.

What you will find as you read through these chapters are two things. First, the market, while being brutally efficient, has inefficiencies that can be exploited over time to generate excess returns. Second, in order to realize these excess returns, an investor must be incredibly patient. You will find that investment strategies which generate alpha have long periods of outperforming and underperforming the market.

For those with the knowledge and the will to persevere this book will show that it is possible to generate excess returns. Let's get started.

# Chapter One

# The Crystal Ball of Wall Street

*Analyst Recommendations and the Future*

IT IS VERY HARD TO PREDICT THE FUTURE. Think about something you like to analyze for fun—such as following the local sports team. In Chicago there are two baseball teams, the White Sox and the Cubs. The two teams face off against each other in what is called the Crosstown Classic. Now no matter how die-hard a Cubs fan you are or what your knowledge of the White Sox is—trying to predict which team will beat the point spread is incredibly difficult. No matter what you think you know about the Cubs, the information is likely reflected in the point spread.

Trying to beat the market is very similar—a stock may in fact be a good buy due to various fundamental reasons, but this information is likely already reflected in the stock's price. If you're trying to select a stock to outperform the market, find a stock for which new information is not currently reflected in the stock's price. Brokerage firms attempt to do this by hiring research analysts.

An investor's first introduction to the work of research analysts is often listening to and acting on a stock recommendation provided by a full-service broker. An investor will purchase a stock because the research analysts at the broker's firm have issued a recommendation to buy. Sometimes a recommended stock will go up, sometimes it will go down. Perhaps the broker will provide a string of prescient recommendations. More likely than not, though, acting on the broker's recommendation will not result in a windfall for the investor. The next logical question for the investor is whether this is because of the broker, the research analysts at the brokerage firm, or simply due to being a small-fry client to the brokerage firm. The answer to this question lies at the heart of the study of investment strategies based on analysts' recommendations.

## Meet the Analyst

Meet Matt, an analyst working at a Wall Street Brokerage firm. Most likely he has graduated from a top-tier MBA program within the past decade or two. Since graduating from business school, Matt has been following the same group of 10 stocks in the enterprise software sector. Unlike an analyst who works for a mutual fund and who has to be moderately familiar with a large number of stocks, Matt is likely one of five or six people in the country who is an expert on the 10 enterprise software companies that he follows.

Matt spends his time researching the companies he follows, meeting with the senior level management, analyzing the industry, and trying to predict which of the companies will be successful. He often talks directly with high-level investors regarding the prospects of the companies that he follows, and he writes extensive research reports on what's going on with them.

The research reports written by analysts like Matt usually contain an estimate of what a company is going to earn on a per-share basis over the next two fiscal years; an estimate of how fast the company is expected to grow its earnings over the next five years; a recommendation of whether an investor should buy, hold, or sell the stock; a target price indicating what the analyst feels the stock should trade at over the next year; and lastly, a detailed explanation illustrating how these results are derived. The report usually contains a spreadsheet that shows the financial estimates behind the earnings projection, and it can be anywhere from a few pages to a short treatise to a semiannual opus.

These research reports are then provided to investors by the brokerage firm in exchange for trading revenue. This means that retail and individual investors who execute trades through a brokerage firm usually can access the firm's proprietary equity research.

However, many retail investors do not spend the time and effort to actually read the report; instead they tend to focus on the recommendation of the report and blindly follow the advice. Unfortunately, this is far from the best way to use the research.

## Listen—But Only if Simon Says "Change"

The purpose of the recommendation is to boil down the fundamental research of the analyst into one actionable suggestion. Do you buy, hold, or sell a stock? Unfortunately, the answer is not always clear. Here's a hint if you want the Cliff's Notes version: Focus on recent recommendation changes from analysts with good track records in small-cap stocks.

Analysts in the United States are collectively paid more than $7 billion each year to tell investors which stocks to buy and which to sell. At the most basic level, there has to be some value to the research analysts' work. If there was not any value in the work, it is unlikely that investment banks, which are usually focused on the bottom line, would continue to pay analysts so much. Research seems to back this up—the analyst recommendations are useful in certain ways.

—————————————————— ∽ ——————————————————

Analysts in the United States are collectively paid more than $7 billion each year to tell investors which stocks to buy and which to sell. At the most basic level there has to be some value to the research analysts' work. If there was not any value in the work, it is unlikely that investment banks, which are usually focused on the bottom line, would continue to pay analysts so much.

There are a few firms worldwide that track analyst recommendations and their performance in the marketplace. One such company is my firm, Zacks Investment Research. In fact, we were the first firm in the country to begin tracking analyst recommendations; as a result, our database of recommendations has the longest history of any company, dating back to the early 1980s.

Research shows that:

1. Changes in analysts' recommendations can be used profitably. The key here is whether an analyst has provided new information to the marketplace by changing his view on a stock.
2. Transaction costs can dramatically reduce the return of recommendation-based strategies.
3. Changes in analysts' recommendations work better with smaller companies (that is, smaller capitalization stocks).
4. You can make more money by using recommendation changes in combination with other criteria.
5. Some analysts tend to have a greater effect on stock prices than others. One way to determine which analyst to follow is to track the analyst's historical accuracy in making stock recommendations.

After roughly two decades of research it looks like analysts' recommendations can be used profitably if the focus is on changes in recommendations as opposed to the level of the recommendation. It is more important if an analyst has recently changed his recommendation than if the analyst has been indicating a stock is a strong buy for the six months.

## Tale of the Tape

One of the simplest investment strategies is to create portfolios based upon what analysts are recommending. That is, you buy the stocks the analyst tells you to buy and sell the stocks the analyst tells you to sell. The basic idea here is that the analyst's recommendation has some predictive ability—that is, those stocks an analyst recommends as a buy should outperform, while those stocks an analyst recommends as a sell should underperform.

Let's say that every calendar quarter you sort all the stocks for which analysts have issued recommendations for into two groups. The first group consists of the top 10 percent of stocks for which analysts are the most positive, and the second group consists of the bottom 10 percent of stocks for which analysts are the most negative. You buy and hold each portfolio for a quarter, and then you create the portfolios again next quarter with new data. From 1990 through 2010, the basket of stocks for which analysts were the most positive outperformed the basket of stocks for which analysts were the least positive in 14 of the 21 years. The strategy of going long stocks recommended by analysts and shorting the stocks analysts indicated you should avoid worked from 1990 to 1997, but then the strategy fell apart.

Let's repeat the experiment from before. This time, instead of sorting the stocks based on the level of recommendations, sort the stocks into 10 groups based on the changes in recommendations that occur over the last month before the end of the quarter.

The good portfolio consists of the top 10 percent of stocks receiving the strongest magnitude of recommendation upgrades over the past month, and the bad portfolio consists of the bottom 10 percent of stocks that are receiving the largest magnitude of recommendation downgrades. In this case, examining the same time period as before, from 1990 through 2010, the basket of stocks consisting of those stocks receiving strong recommendation upgrades outperformed the basket receiving substantial recommendation downgrades in 19 of the past 21 years.

Results become even stronger when the creation of the portfolios is closer to the time of the recommendation changes. Studies have shown that excess returns increase substantially when the rebalance frequency—the period in which you are creating the basket of stocks based on changes in recommendations—is shifted from monthly to weekly, and it increases again when the rebalance frequency is shifted to daily. However, the data show that the returns from recommendation-based strategies are very volatile over time and are highly dependent on transaction costs.

Effectively, with recommendation-based strategies it's a crapshoot whether any given year will be profitable for the strategy. This means that statistically over time the strategy of focusing on changes in analysts' recommendations should generate market-beating returns, but any given year could result in positive excess returns or negative excess returns relative to a simple buy and hold strategy. Because of this volatility, it is necessary when employing recommendation-based strategies to try to implement the strategy through a full market cycle measured in years, not months.

## Paying the Tolls

The other issue with recommendation-based strategies concerns transaction costs. Transaction costs can be broken down into four major categories:

1. Commissions
2. Bid/ask spreads
3. Price impact
4. Liquidity costs

First and foremost are the actual commissions that an investor has to pay for transacting in stocks. If you buy a share of stock through a discount online brokerage firm, your account will be charged a flat commission. For example, you are charged $9.99 for executing a trade through any one of a dozen online brokerage firms.

Institutional investors are charged commissions, but they are often quoted as a certain number of cents per share traded. Institutional commissions are also constantly moving lower; currently it is not unheard of for an institutional investor to pay a fraction of a penny per share in commission costs.

However, commissions can be seen as only the tip in an iceberg of costs and frictions involved in stock transactions. Much more pernicious is a whole slew of costs such as the bid/ask spreads, price impact, and liquidity costs that represent a much larger portion of transaction costs. When the full iceberg of transaction costs is considered—not just the commission tip sticking out of the water—it is clear that trading strategies based on recommendations should seek to minimize the turnover or frequency of transactions.

For instance, a recent study of a recommendation-based trading strategy, where an investor would simply buy those companies with the best recommendations, shows an annualized abnormal return of 9.4 percent. However, after accounting for transaction costs, the excess annual return falls to −3.1 percent.

Studies of recommendation data that try to incorporate transaction costs are quite controversial, simply because there is no accepted means of estimating transaction costs.

The estimate of transaction costs tends to decrease over time as information technology improves. The transaction costs incurred for buying stocks in 1982 were higher than those incurred in 2002, which in turn were higher than in 2010. Additionally, investment strategies that focus on the level of analyst recommendations tend to be relatively unpredictable in the returns they generate. It is not uncommon to see results swing dramatically from year to year with no change in the criteria used for portfolio creation. Thus the risk-adjusted return of pure recommendation-based strategies tends to be lower than that for other investment anomalies.

## Smaller is Better

Practically all studies of recommendation-based investment strategies indicate that the excess return of the strategies remains concentrated in small firms. A firm's size refers to its market capitalization or the aggregate value of its equity. Small firms are usually, but not always, followed by fewer analysts.

The reason small-cap stocks respond better to recommendation changes could be that the market is less efficient for smaller firms and the amount of information is more limited. Another possibility is that the higher transaction costs for smaller firms prevent large institutional traders from trading in the small-cap stocks and eliminating the excess returns due to the recommendation changes. This does not appear to be unique for recommendation-based trading strategies—most anomalies seem to work better in smaller-cap stocks. The key is whether the excess returns continue to persist after adjusting for the transaction costs.

## Combo Attacks

For even better returns, we can try combining information by using analyst recommendations with other fundamental data. For instance, a recent study showed that if you buy stocks with positive recommendations, the excess returns generated are higher when you also combine the additional factors of high price momentum, attractive valuation multiples and high earnings quality. Additionally, by incorporating other fundamental criteria, it is possible to reduce the overall turnover of recommendation-based strategies. If a stock's valuation multiple is attractive, the valuation multiple tends to remain attractive for at least several quarters. Recommendation changes tend to be more fleeting. A stock cannot continue to receive substantial recommendation upgrades quarter after quarter, because after one or two quarters analysts are unanimously recommending the stock as a buy with no room for upgrades.

Interestingly enough, it appears that recommendation optimism tends to increase with both price and earnings momentum. That is, those companies whose prices have been going up and who have been strongly growing their earnings are more likely to be highly recommended by analysts. If analysts were focused only upon valuation, one would expect the opposite to be the case. Another indication that price momentum may lead to analyst recommendation upgrades is that more favorable recommendations are often associated with less favorable valuation metrics.

This means that momentum stocks and stocks that tend to be expensive are more likely to be highly recommended by analysts. For this reason, some of the results attributed to analyst recommendation studies may be the result of a price momentum anomaly. However, many of the studies address this issue by using a model of expected returns that incorporates price momentum. Buying pure price momentum is not a bad strategy, but it requires high turnover and short holding periods. This leads me to believe that recommendation-based strategies should almost always incorporate a fundamental valuation factor as well—otherwise an investor could very likely be simply buying in-vogue momentum stocks.

It also appears that following large stock price increases, analysts are just as likely to either upgrade or downgrade their recommendation; however, following large stock price decreases, analysts are much more likely to downgrade a stock.

Investors tend to be risk-averse when dealing with gains, but willing to take on more risk when facing losses. This behavioral bias makes retail investors willing to bear more risk when dealing with losses. As a result, retail investors tend to underreact when there is a major downward move in a stock. Effectively they become averse to realizing losses and instead chose to increase risk by keeping their position open.

Basically, investors look to add risk with losses, so they are more likely to continue to hold a stock if it is below their purchase price. In order to correct this bias it may help to listen to stock analysts. Effectively, by selling on a recommendation downgrade following a large negative price movement it may help an investor combat the behavioral bias that would lead him to continue to hold the stock.

## The Good, the Bad, and the Ugly

Some very recent research also indicates that those analysts who have a good track record historically for making recommendations tend to issue better performing recommendations. One trading strategy found that an investor who follows the recommendations of analysts in the top 10 percent with respect to performance in the previous quarter would tend to generate excess returns. It appears that the best analysts tend to persist for two quarters following the rankings of such analysts. This could be due either to underlying price momentum in the securities or perhaps to the informational advantages afforded to certain analysts.

Further research indicates that stock recommendations by analysts who attended the same university as members of the board of directors of corporations they are following tend to be more accurate. However, this study analyzed a period prior to the passage of Regulation Fair Disclosure (Reg FD). This regulation requires publicly traded companies to divulge market-moving information to everyone at the same time. This is usually accomplished through press releases. It effectively limited the selective disclosure of information to privileged analysts, and in effect it helped level the playing field. As a result of Reg FD, all analysts must receive the same information at the same time.

So who exactly is using analyst recommendations in making investment decisions? It is clear that both individual and institutional investors react to the actual recommendation announcements. Further parsing of the data has shown that individuals trade more on recommendation upgrades, and institutional investors tend to focus more on recommendation downgrades. This makes sense, since generally a recommendation upgrade can be used as fodder for a brokerage firm's sales force to induce more people to buy a certain security, while a recommendation downgrade is of interest only to those investors who already hold the given stock.

---~---

**Further parsing of the data has shown that individuals trade more on recommendation upgrades, and institutional investors tend to focus more on recommendation downgrades.**

---

As a result of this distinction between who trades on recommendation upgrades and downgrades, it seems that recommendation downgrades are more informative, since the more sophisticated investor bases trades on them. The reason behind this result is simple: Institutions tend to be more sophisticated than individuals. As a result, an individual should mimic the trading behavior of institutions and pay more attention to recommendation downgrades than recommendation upgrades. Basically, individuals should pay more attention when an analyst downgrades rather than upgrades a stock.

Several studies show an increase in institutional trading volume around the time recommendations are publicly released. This suggests that recommendation changes are important to institutional investors. The net takeaway?

Recommendations do move markets, institutions trade on changes in recommendations, and downgrades are more important than upgrades.

Furthermore, trading on analyst recommendations is a global opportunity. Examining the effectiveness of using recommendation data in seven large markets shows that recommendation changes are most profitable in the United States and Japan. Positive results are also found in France and Canada as well. Other markets in which recommendation changes tend to provide some value are India, Brazil, and Australia. Almost all the international studies seem to verify what the U.S. domestic studies show: Namely, changes in recommendation data are far more important than recommendation levels.

## Making It Part of Your Process

So how can we use recommendation data in an investment process? Consider the following facts:

1. Changes in recommendations are far more important than the level of recommendations.
2. Recommendation downgrades are more important than recommendation upgrades.
3. Investment strategies using recommendation changes are more effective among small-cap stocks.

4. Recommendation changes should be combined with fundamental data in order to reduce transaction costs and generate better returns.

These facts combined with the results of the transaction-cost tests indicate that although excess returns can be generated from following changes in recommendations, the strategy should be used in conjunction with other methodologies. While focusing on recommendation changes seems to be an effective investment anomaly, it is plagued by higher turnover, which, if an investor is not careful, could eat deeply into the returns. As we shall see in later chapters, there are other more effective strategies that can be implemented. It is useful to use recommendations with additional strategies in order to lower the turnover.

For instance, a simple test within the 3,000 largest cap stocks demonstrates the power of using recommendation changes in an investment strategy in combination with a valuation metric. If we rebalance quarterly and we combine recommendation changes and valuation metrics, we find excess returns can be generated with relatively reasonable degrees of turnover.

# Chapter Two

# Size Matters

~

*How Owning Small-Cap Stocks
Can Mean Big Rewards*

IF YOU ASK ANY RECENT MBA STUDENT FOR A MEANS OF selecting stocks to outperform the market, he will indicate that a sure-fire method lies in buying small-capitalization (or small-cap) stocks. For the past 30 years, students have been taught that a basket of stocks with low market capitalization will generate greater returns than a basket of stocks of the big well-established companies.

What exactly is "small-cap" and what is "large-cap"? Well, let's start with asking this: What is market capitalization and how do you slice it? Market capitalization is what the stock market says a company is worth. Market capitalization is determined by multiplying the current price of a single share by the total number of outstanding shares of stock. Since most indexes that rank companies are weighted by market capitalization, it's important to know how the index defines the different market capitalization categories. Generally, small-cap is defined as a company with market capitalization below $2 billion. Large-cap usually represents companies with a market cap above $10 billion.

## Bigger Isn't Necessarily Better

When analyzing small-cap versus large-cap stocks, we'll look at two things: return and risk. The returns part is pretty straightforward. While a basket of small-cap stocks might not generate higher returns than a basket of large-cap stocks every single year, on average you make more money over time by holding the small-cap stocks. This phenomenon was first documented in 1981 by a young professor, Rolf Banz, at the University of Chicago.

What Banz did was program a computer to sort all the stocks in a database into quintiles—or five equal groups—each year. He then looked at how each group performed over the next year and then resorted the stocks at the end of that year.

The findings were pretty astonishing. Those stocks that were in the bottom 20 percent of the firms as ranked by market capitalization generated annualized yearly returns that were almost 5 percent higher than the returns of the larger-cap stocks. Immediately another researcher confirmed this effect by using a broader sample of stocks and sorting the stocks into deciles based on market capitalization.

It was pretty exciting stuff. No matter how you sliced and measured the equity market capitalization pie, it looked like you made more money by eating the smaller pieces. Let them eat crumbs was the verdict of the academics—the smaller the better. Firms were founded and fortunes minted based on this observation. Billions of dollars of pension fund money started to find a new home among a nascent group of growing small-cap managers. People started buying all the small-cap stocks indiscriminately. Own them all, the belief went, no matter how small, and the returns will be greater.

Then, just as the entire professional money management industry revved up to exploit the anomaly, something strange occurred—the anomaly disappeared. Not just for a couple of years but for two full decades.

For the next 20 years small-cap stocks generated about the same return as large-cap stocks, with more risk. As I indicated, the return part is pretty easy to measure: From 1981 to 2001, did you make more money in the large-cap or small-cap stocks? The risk part requires a little explanation.

When researchers discuss the risks of holding stocks there is a disconnect between the measurement of risk and the intuitive understanding of risk by an investor. Risk is usually measured by looking at the standard deviation of the returns. This means a lot if you have a good understanding of statistics but is lost on the street-smart investor. Standard deviation really means how much the returns are different over time from what is expected to occur. An investment strategy that generates big losses and big gains is deemed to be more risky than a strategy that generates consistent returns.

The street-smart investor sees risk differently. To most investors, risk is the chance of a bad outcome materializing. Risk is not determined by whether a bad outcome actually occurs; rather, risk is the chance that a bad outcome *may* occur. If you walk across a rickety bridge but don't fall into the gorge, you are enduring risk even though you got across the bridge.

The problem is that what potentially could happen cannot be measured. You can't look at small-cap stocks in 2005 and ask what returns might have materialized with the basket of small-cap stocks. All you can observe is what actually did occur in 2005 with small-cap stocks. Risk, then, as measured by the statistician, boils down to seeing whether something different occurs every year or if the same thing happens every year. There is a huge problem with this way of looking at the world.

~

**Standard deviation really means how much the returns are different over time from what is expected to occur. An investment strategy that generates big losses and big gains is deemed to be more risky than a strategy that generates consistent returns.**

Let's say you want to make some unusual bets on Chicago White Sox baseball games. You believe that the Sox have a great defense, and it's not very likely that the total runs scored by the visiting and home team combined will ever exceed 24. So you go to Las Vegas in 2006 and, sure enough, there is a bookmaker named Louie who will take your bet with one caveat: If you enter into the bet, for every regular season game where the total runs scored in a game do not exceed 24 you win $100, but if the total runs scored equals or exceeds 25 you lose $100,000. The standard deviation of the returns generated by this gambling strategy would be very constant over time. Historical evidence would suggest that you have an excellent chance of walking away with $16,200 in your pocket at the end of every regular season, and 28 games into the seventh season you would break even. No-brainer, right?

Season after season you sit in your box seat on Chicago's South Side, enjoy a few hot dogs with your peanuts, and count your money. Then, on a hot, sticky, summer night, August 3, 2011, you get your lunch handed to you as Derek Jeter and Curtis Granderson lead the New York Yankees to an 18–7 pounding of your beloved Chicago White Sox. The next morning, your old friend Louie calls and he wants his money.

Simply looking at the standard deviation of returns over an historical period led you to believe it was a low risk bet. In reality, the bet was akin to picking up quarters in front of an oncoming steamroller; you made a little money until you got crushed.

The point is that risk is very hard to measure if all you're looking at is history without understanding the process that generates the returns. Selling naked puts on the S&P 500 could generate phenomenal risk-adjusted return numbers, but it is effectively taking a bet where there is a small likelihood of horrible negative returns and a large likelihood of small positive returns. Unless the horrible return occurs, the data would indicate a low-risk strategy.

So the question of whether small-cap stocks generate excess risk-adjusted returns really can only be answered by determining why small-cap stocks should generate higher returns than large-cap stocks. If you don't understand why small-cap stocks should generate returns in excess of the risk borne you are left wondering which series of data to believe—the data prior to 1981 or the data after 1981?

## The Tax Man Cometh (or the January Effect)

One reason small-cap stocks might outperform over time has to do with taxes. There is a lot of evidence that to a large extent the outperformance of small-cap stocks in the United States is due to the returns of small-cap stocks in January. This pattern was first noted by investment banker Sidney B. Wachtel, who coined the term "January effect" in his 1942 paper, "Certain Observations on Seasonal Movements in Stock Prices," published in the *Journal of Business* of the University of Chicago.

Why would small-cap stocks deliver much greater returns in January? A cynic might say that it is just random—that January just by chance is the month when small-cap stocks tend to outperform. Another possibility is that small-cap stocks are more likely to be held by individuals and entities that need to pay taxes. The large pension fund likely does not hold many sub-$100 million equities;

rather such small stocks are held by people who have some association with the companies in question.

These individuals not only want to make returns, but also they care about the returns they make after they pay taxes. Because the tax pay period is on a calendar year basis, individuals who hold small-cap stocks may choose to unload the stocks or positions sometime before December in order to generate losses to offset gains or to carry forward for taxes due in April.

True small-cap stocks are generally thinly traded, and if a lot of people want to realize losses, in a given year, small-cap stocks may become overly depressed in price by the beginning of the new calendar year. As a result, the small-cap stocks that have underperformed in the previous year and experienced tax loss selling tend to pop in January, since all the tax-loss selling has depressed prices to a point where greater than market returns can be generated by purchasing them.

Some studies focusing on the pre-1981 period seem to indicate that almost 50 percent of the size effect—or the excess returns generated by holding small-cap stocks—may be due to the January effect. Thus, small-cap stocks outperform, but this is due to some bizarre consequence of the U.S. tax code causing imbalances between buyers and sellers. The whole explanation, while plausible, seems a little too convoluted for my taste, but stranger things have proven true.

## Everybody Loves a Bargain

Another possibility is that the excess returns generated by small-cap stocks actually represent a way of compensating investors for holding illiquid investments. The basic idea is that small-cap stocks are priced at a discount to their fair value because it is so hard to trade them. Although the company's stock is worth $20, you may be able to buy it for $18 because once you own the stock it is very hard to find someone to sell it to. This would not be unheard of in finance; it is very common for financial assets to trade at a liquidity discount, and the idea at first blush passes the commonsense argument.

Research seems to indicate that among the stocks that trade on the NYSE, the excess returns due to small-cap stocks disappear and in some cases actually reverse when transaction costs are taken into account. For instance, some tests show that if you adjust the returns of holding small-cap stocks for the difference between what brokers will buy the stocks at and what they will sell them to investors at, the bid/ask spread essentially eliminates the excess returns generated by small-cap stocks. Generally, though, tests analyzing whether excess returns can be generated by holding small-cap stocks after adjusting for transaction costs have proven to be inconclusive.

No sooner does one study indicate that small-cap excess returns are a function of not adjusting for transaction costs than another analysis shows that the excess returns of small-cap stocks do not disappear when adjusted for transaction costs. Ultimately, with transaction costs falling across the board, the relevance of transaction cost tests done five or even 10 years ago is questionable. The transaction costs are definitely higher for small-cap stocks, but the proof is in the pudding. The ultimate conclusion of whether small-cap stocks outperform large-cap stocks over time can only be determined by observing the results of actual investment over long periods of time. My belief is that over the next 50 years, small-cap stocks should generate greater returns than large-cap stocks.

## How Far Back Should You Look?

Even after adjusting for transaction costs, the biggest problem with the returns generated by owning small-cap stocks is that many times the excess returns seem ephemeral—a shimmering mirage caused by the capriciousness of the market. Much recent research seems to indicate that the strength of the excess returns of owning small-cap stocks varies across different periods of time. Looking at returns from 1980 to 1996 seem to indicate that there is, in effect, no relationship between market capitalization and returns. During this time period there was no advantage to owning small-cap stocks. Note that this is not a few years but a decade and a half, and it corresponds to the decade and a half after the discovery of the small-cap anomaly. Effectively, after being discovered, the excess returns of small-cap stocks went into hibernation.

If we focus on the years from 1982 to 2002, the excess returns due to owning small-cap stocks were much smaller than during the period 1926 to 1982. The explanation for this clearly is that the decline in excess returns from owning small-cap stocks may be due to the impact from the various papers that discussed the small-cap anomaly and the acceptance of the small-cap anomaly as gospel by the professional investment community.

While it is somewhat a coincidence that the excess returns due to small-cap stocks seemed to disappear right after their discovery, another possible explanation is just pure randomness. It is also quite possible that something fundamental occurred in the economy over the past 20 years that gave an advantage to large-cap stocks. Looking at data from 1984 to 2005, excess returns due to small-cap stocks fell to an annualized rate of about 1 percent per year over large-cap stocks. This excess performance is so small that for all practical purposes small-cap stocks performed roughly in line with large-cap stocks. While these results are nothing new, what is interesting is a potential explanation. One reason small-cap stocks may have underperformed has to do with the fact that small-cap stocks experienced greater negative profitability shocks. Prior to 1984, profitability shocks—which are basically unexpected earnings changes that reduce profitability—were very close to zero for all size deciles. However, starting in 1984, small firms on average experienced negative profitability shocks while big firms experienced positive profitability shocks. As a result, it is possible that the realized returns on small firms were lower than the expected returns. Essentially, small-cap stocks had a bad run of luck for the last 20 years—but the distribution these returns are realized from remains higher than the distribution of returns for large-cap stocks. In my mind this is a relatively likely explanation.

Over long periods of time (think multiple decades), small-cap stocks should outperform. However, over any decade or two it is very possible that small-cap stocks will underperform their large-cap brethren.

In fact, if the period being examined is 1983 to 1998, you find that small-cap stocks underperformed large-cap stocks by about 40 percent. About this time many researchers began to question the existence of the small-cap anomaly. However, no sooner was the ability of small-cap stocks to outperform large-cap stocks questioned than, lo and behold, for the next 10 years—1999 to 2010—small-cap stocks substantially outperformed large-cap stocks.

Looking at the full period of 1927 through 2010, we find small-caps outperforming in certain years and under-performing in other years. The data looks very stationary, which means that there does not seem to be a pattern of outperformance. In any given year it looks like performance can go either way in regard to small- or large-caps.

One interesting tidbit of data is that the period from 1983 to 1998 showed the worst string of performance for small-cap stocks since reliable data have been recorded. So the question of whether the small-cap anomaly exists boils down to what is the base case? Should we focus on the data before 1981, or do we examine the data from 1981 to 1998, or perhaps the data from 1998 to 2010. The existence of the small-cap anomaly is therefore highly dependent on the period being examined. What is very clear is that since being widely publicized in the early 1980s, small-cap stocks have not done as well as expected.

Another interesting thing about the size anomaly is that it owes much of the excess return to truly small-cap stocks. Eugene Fama and Kenneth French, fathers of the famous Fama-French three-factor model to describe market behavior, show through a sophisticated way of sorting stocks by capitalization that the smaller the market capitalization of a stock, the greater the stock's contribution to excess returns by market capitalization. This could potentially point towards stale pricing as a determinant of excess return by small capitalization stocks.

It also looks like earnings surprises play a role in generating small-cap excess returns. The bulk of the excess returns of small-cap stocks is attributable to firms that have a history of generating sub-par earnings relative to expectations. Results tend to support the behavioral hypothesis that investors collectively overreact to bad news by overselling stocks with poor earnings performance. Effectively, it looks like small-cap excess returns may be driven by a lack of interest among institutional investors for relatively small, unknown stocks that have fallen dramatically in price.

One very good way to test whether a pattern of stock price performance such as small-cap stocks outperforming large-cap stocks will hold in the future is to determine the results hold within a country that did not serve as the basis for the original result. If the small-cap phenomenon is discovered in the United States but then we find that in foreign markets small-cap stocks consistently underperform, it may be an indication that the initial observation is simply due to randomness.

Additional studies looking at international markets seem to indicate that something is occurring among small-cap stocks and that the small-cap phenomenon is likely real. Out of 12 European countries examined, smaller-cap stocks tended to generate higher average returns in 11 of them. The results hold if the Canadian Stock Market is looked at as well. Examining companies that trade on the 20 emerging stock markets shows that an internationally diversified portfolio of small stocks outperforms a similarly diversified portfolio of large stocks by about 70 basis points per month without adjusting for transaction costs.

So what does all the data add up to? First, it does appear that over long stretches of time you can outperform the market by holding smaller-cap stocks. However, you must be very patient through decades, and over any 5- or 10-year period it is very possible that large-caps will outperform small-caps. To exploit the small-cap anomaly, you truly need to have a long-term time horizon. Additionally, it appears that transaction costs can eat up a large portion of returns among small-cap stocks, so it is relatively important to keep turnover at a minimum.

～

**What does all the data add up to? First, it does appear that over long stretches of time you can outperform the market by holding smaller-cap stocks. However, you must be very patient through decades, and over any 5- or 10-year period it is very possible that large-caps will outperform small-caps.**

## No News Can Be Great News

Finally, it is likely the case that the excess returns due to holding small-cap stocks come primarily from neglected companies. These are small-cap stocks that tend to be subject to the January effect, stocks for which an investor base is hard to find, and stocks that have historically disappointed investors. The behavioral analysis of overreaction to bad news seems to hold water.

This belief in overreaction to bad news makes sense when you realize that small-cap stocks are, for most institutional investors, largely unknown. As a result of this lack of familiarity, institutional investors may have a much harder time finding value in small-cap stocks. For instance, if GE sells off by a large percentage amount, there are many investors who would realize that the sell-off is overdone and GE represents a value at the given price. This occurs because large numbers of investors spend massive amounts of time and money analyzing GE's prospects. Also, GE has extensive analyst coverage. If, however, a $100 million market capitalization stock were to sell off by a large amount, there would not be the same amount of money as a percentage of market capitalization basis that is following the small-cap company, due primarily to a lack of information. As a result, there may be systematic overreaction to bad news with regard to small-cap stocks. This would potentially cause small-cap stocks in aggregate to remain unduly depressed following price pullbacks and thus generate returns that are in excess of the market. Effectively, because of the lack of institutional interest, when small-cap stocks hit the canvas they can be slow to get back up.

## Good Things in Small Packages

It appears that if you are going to try to exploit the small-cap anomaly, small-cap value is the way to go. Such investors look for beaten down stocks that are trading at attractive valuations and are relatively unknown to the larger investing public.

However, it is extremely important to be patient or even to some degree stubborn. If you enter into buying small-cap stocks you must try to stay the course through at least a decade in order to generate any excess return. If your level of belief in small-cap stocks is not high and unwavering, you stand the risk of buying small-caps when they are in favor and selling them when small-caps are out of favor. Thus, the returns generated will be substantially below the returns generated from a historical analysis of the period over which you invest.

In order to make money investing in small-cap stocks it requires a commitment to the belief that over time small-cap stocks will outperform large-cap stocks. The reason this belief is necessary is that more likely than not at some point in time there will be a large period in which small-cap stocks underperform large-cap stocks.

Examining the international data, it is very likely that over the long-haul small-cap stocks will prevail. The problem is that all the data seems to indicate that to truly profit from the small-cap phenomenon you need to hold small-cap stocks for multiple decades. This is by no means easy to accomplish but those investors able to buy and hold small-cap stocks and stay invested over long periods of time will likely generate returns that are greater than the market.

# Chapter Three

# Once More Unto the Breach

~

*The Art of Deciphering Earnings Estimates*

THE STOCK MARKET IS A PRETTY SIMPLE CONCEPT ON THE face of it. You have the sell-side of the market, which are the institutions focused on selling financial assets and securities. The sell-side consists primarily of the banks, brokers, dealers, and investment bankers whose job it is to sell securities to their customers. On the buy-side of the market, you have institutions concerned with buying, rather than selling, assets or securities. Pension funds, mutual funds, foundations, hedge funds, endowments, and proprietary trading desks are the most common types of buy-side entities.

A company requires capital in order to produce and market its products. In order to raise that capital, it goes to the market and arranges for a sell-side entity to sell fractional shares of ownership in the company, which are represented by stock certificates. The stock market is simply a way of facilitating the transfer of capital from those who have it to those who need it. Effectively, the stock market is a method of pricing the capital on a regular basis so those who contribute the capital can recognize some degree of liquidity.

What ultimately gives a company's stock value are the earnings the company generates. At the end of the day a stock's value is completely determined by the potential cash flows that are due to the owner of the stock. These potential cash flows are usually in the form of dividends but the key here is potential cash flows. The potential dividend payments are what give a stock value. The size of the potential dividend payments is driven by whether the underlying company behind the stock is generating earnings. A profitable company is a company that can pay dividends in the future. For this reason, future earnings ultimately drive a stock's value.

Without earnings, stocks are simply pretty pieces of paper with elaborate designs on them. With earnings, and especially with growth in earnings, stocks have some intrinsic value.

Because future earnings are incredibly important in determining a stock's value, earnings estimates become extraordinarily important.

Earnings estimates reflect the market's best guess at what the future earnings of a company are going to be. At the end of the day the most powerful force driving stock prices are future earnings. While the market's expectations of future earnings are not known, what is observable are the earnings estimates made by sell-side equity

---

Earnings estimates reflect the market's best guess at what the future earnings of a company are going to be. At the end of the day the most powerful force driving stock prices are future earnings. While the market's expectations of future earnings are not known, what is observable are the earnings estimates made by sell-side equity analysts. For this reason, earnings estimates drive stock prices.

analysts. For this reason, earnings estimates drive stock prices.

## In the Beginning There Was the Valuation Model

Most institutional investors use valuation models that have projected corporate earnings as their primary input. While the quality and stability of future earnings must be accounted for, almost all institutional valuation models attempt to find the current value of the future earnings stream by discounting future earnings by an appropriate discount rate. If the discounted value of future earnings is above a company's current share price, the company's stock will be considered a buy. Similarly, if the discounted value of future earnings is below a company's current share price, the company's stock is considered overvalued and the stock will likely be considered a sell candidate.

While the valuation models that run off future earnings estimates can be highly sophisticated or relatively simple, all of them are driven by earnings estimates. Across all institutional valuation models, higher projected earnings result in a higher fair value of the stock. When large institutional investors raise their estimates of future earnings, the institutional investors are much more likely to buy the stock.

A mutual fund company like Fidelity is a buy-side entity, which means their research and earnings estimates are not published for the individual investor to use. If you want to know which stocks a Fidelity portfolio manager is likely to be buying, find a list of the companies Fidelity believes are worth more now than they were one month ago. If Fidelity believes the company is worth more than its current stock price, it will buy the stock. Fidelity however has no reason to provide you with an indication a company is undervalued until they actually buy the stock. The research Fidelity performs is not published.

Unlike the analysts who work at Fidelity, the analysts who work at brokerage houses do publish their research. The research produced by a major brokerage firm like Merrill Lynch is provided to firms like Fidelity in exchange for trading revenue. Because the sell-side firm has many clients like Fidelity, it can effectively afford to hire many more analysts than Fidelity. What has developed over the years is that the in-depth analysis is concentrated at the sell-side firms because of economies of scale. As a result, each sell-side analyst may cover a handful of stocks for their entire career.

The sell-side analyst becomes an expert on the firms he covers and is the person the buy-side analysts turn to in order to gain an accurate prediction of a company's future earnings. The buy-side analyst is responsible for using the research produced by the sell-side analyst to effectively determine which stocks to recommend that the portfolio manager buy. The sell-side analyst knows everything under the sun about maybe 10 companies, all of which are in the same industry. The buy-side analyst is then responsible for using the research from multiple sell-side analysts, each of whom is an expert on a relatively narrow industry and a handful of stocks to help create a portfolio.

As a result, buy-side firms' estimates of corporate earnings are driven by the sell-side research reports. This is what makes sell-side research so important—the earnings estimates produced by the sell-side are used as inputs on the buy-side. When a sell-side analyst raises his earnings estimates these higher estimates are used by the buy-side as inputs into their valuation models. The higher the earnings estimates, the higher the valuation model indicates as a fair value for the stock, and the more likely a large institutional investor is to buy the stock.

Because the research of the analysts who work at brokerage firms is widely distributed and used by large institutional investment managers, upward revisions of earnings estimates should lead to upward revisions of fundamental valuations and to a rising stock price. For this reason, the earnings estimates issued by analysts are the most important piece of information produced by equity research analysts.

Luckily for investors, earnings estimates are also the most unbiased research produced by analysts as well as their most frequent output. Any analyst who has been working on Wall Street for an extended period of time can provide a compelling argument why a certain stock is a buy or a sell. The recommendation the analyst provides is inherently biased. For example, an analyst does not want to upset the management of the company he is following, in fear of being cut off from the information flow. As a result, analysts are generally unlikely to issue sell recommendations. Similarly, an analyst may be overly excited about the industry he has spent his career following. An analyst who has spent his life covering publicly traded newspaper companies has a hard time writing research reports indicating that his extensive knowledge of the newspaper industry is about to become useless because the companies are coming under pressure from the Internet.

## The Unbiased Tether . . .

While recommendations of any kind are biased, analysts' earnings estimates are, for the most part, tethered to reality. Each calendar quarter every company must report earnings and the analyst must try to predict those earnings. Regardless of what the analyst thinks about the stock, the industry, or the analyst's contribution to the revenue at the firm where he works, the analyst must provide an accurate estimate of the company's earnings.

Although an analyst's earnings estimates are the least biased part of the research report produced by a sell-side analyst, forecasts are not without their problems. Studies have clearly shown that analysts' earnings estimates are too optimistic. If you look at all changes in earnings estimates over multiple years you find that there are more downward revisions of earnings estimates than upward revisions. Why? Well, after years of covering the same companies, analysts naturally want the companies they are covering to do well. If the company the analyst is covering starts to grow earnings greater than expectations, the analyst's research starts to become greater in demand. In other words, the analyst will often start to drink the Kool-Aid and begin to believe management's statements that earnings will improve. Think of it as a financial version of Stockholm Syndrome—the analyst becomes the captive of the company's management adopting its optimistic earnings bias.

Additionally, analysts tend to be easily swayed by earnings that come from accruals as opposed to cash. Think of accrual earnings as earnings due to increases in balance sheet items as opposed to cold, hard cash. Effectively analysts, like investors, tend to believe earnings due to accruals will persist and as a result tend to err on the optimistic side with respect to earnings estimates.

As we will see later on in Chapter 9, analysts also tend not to fully incorporate the results of earnings announcements in making their estimates.

Despite these drawbacks, using earnings estimate revisions to select stocks remains one of the best means of generating excess returns over time.

## A Consensus of Opinions

The key to using earnings estimate revisions in an investment process is not to focus on the changes made by any one individual analyst. Rather, an investor should focus on the changes made by multiple analysts over time. You want to buy stocks that are receiving upward earnings estimate revisions from multiple analysts, and avoid or sell stocks that are receiving downward earnings estimate revisions by multiple analysts.

------------------------------ ∾ ------------------------------

**The key to using earnings estimate revisions in an investment process is not to focus on the changes made by any one individual analyst. Rather, an investor should focus on the changes made by multiple analysts over time.**

It is pretty clear that the market underreacts to earnings estimate revisions. The reason this occurs is that earnings estimate revisions are serially correlated over time. What this means is that stocks that have received multiple upward earnings estimate revisions are more likely to receive upward earnings estimate revisions in the future. By buying companies that have received upward earnings estimate revisions in the past you are purchasing the stock of companies that are statistically more likely to receive upward earnings estimate revisions in the future.

When these upward earnings estimate revisions actually materialize, the market responds to them as the valuation models used by large institutional investors show a higher fair value due to the higher estimates used as an input. This results in more investors buying the stock and having the stock price rise.

Thus, in using earnings estimate revisions, the ability to generate excess returns really boils down to predicting which companies will receive upward earnings estimate revisions as well as determining whether prices will respond to the anticipated upward earnings estimate revisions. Predicting which companies are likely to receive upward earnings estimate revisions is a statistical question. However, determining which companies' stock prices will respond to future earnings estimate revisions is more of an art. Both need to work in unison in order to effectively generate excess returns.

From the available research, we know that hedged portfolios structured on earnings estimate revisions generate positive returns. A portfolio consisting of being long the top 5 percent of all stocks based on earnings estimate revisions and short the bottom 5 percent of all stocks based on earnings estimate revisions generates annualized return in the neighborhood of 10 percent per year gross of transaction costs. Studies show that these market neutral returns based on earnings estimate revisions tend to persist over time. Research studies done throughout the 1970s, 1980s, and 1990s all show positive and statistically significant excess returns. These results are consistent with a market that responds slowly or underreacts to earnings estimate revisions.

Many studies have looked into what company characteristics tend to enhance the value of earnings estimate revisions. Results seem to indicate that earnings estimate revisions are more profitable among smaller companies and companies with fewer analysts.

It also appears that earnings estimate revisions have greater value when the earnings estimate revision is away from the consensus. For instance, if the average earnings estimate of all the analysts following a stock is $1.05, an earnings estimate revision from $1.05 to $1.10 is a more powerful predictor of future price appreciation than an earnings estimate revision from $1.00 to $1.05. In this example, although both potential earnings estimate revisions would change the consensus estimate by the same amount, the move that is from the consensus to above the consensus is a more powerful predictor of future price performance than the earnings estimate revision that is from below the consensus to the consensus.

The bolder the earnings estimate revision, the greater the degree of investor underreaction to the estimate revision and the more powerful the earnings estimate revision is in predicting future price movement. For this reason, large earnings estimate revisions as a percentage of the consensus estimate tend to have a greater impact on future price performance. If the consensus earnings estimate is $1.00, an earnings estimate revision of $0.30 has a greater impact than an earnings estimate revision of $0.10.

Why would investors tend to underreact more to bold earnings estimate revisions? Part of the explanation is that investors are potentially waiting for confirmation from additional earnings estimate revisions from other analysts or confirmation from reported actual earnings before changing their own view of the firm's earnings prospects. In fact, a significant portion of the excess returns that follow an earnings estimate revision tends to materialize around additional earnings estimate revisions or actual reported quarterly earnings. This seems to indicate that part of the reason for underreaction to earnings estimate revisions revolves around an investor's need to obtain confirmation of a new earnings view from additional sources.

## Sources of Change

Last year, there were roughly 180,000 earnings estimate revisions made by more than 3,500 analysts employed in the United States. If you analyze the analysts, and look at earnings estimate revisions over multiple years—which entails examining more than a million earnings estimate revisions—you can try to statistically determine what might be causing the analysts to pull the trigger and change their earnings estimates.

It definitely appears that analysts are more likely to revise a company's earnings estimates upward if the company's stock price has recently risen. Most likely, this is because both the stock price and the earnings estimate are being driven by new fundamental information. Analysts are also more likely to revise their earnings estimates upward just after an earnings announcement or a corporate meeting—again this is an example of new information about a stock being analyzed and leading to earnings estimate revisions. Finally, data shows that analysts tend to revise their earnings estimates in the same direction of recent dividend changes. That is, if a company just recently raised its dividend, analysts appear likely to revise their earnings estimates upward following the increase in dividend.

Most importantly, analysts tend to herd with regard to their earnings estimate revisions. What this means is that analysts are likely to be revising their earnings estimates upward if other analysts are also revising upward. Analysts behave to some degree like lemmings making their earnings estimate revisions together.

A recent statistical analysis that was conducted by Professor George Serafeim of Harvard and detailed in the *Handbook of Equity Market Anomalies*, examines determinants of earnings estimate revisions. The study shows that there are probably five factors that contribute to an analyst making a revision to his or her earnings estimates. Think of these factors as the trigger or tipping point that causes analysts to revise their earnings estimates.

Roughly 54 percent of the changes in earnings estimates can be explained by these five factors. The other 46 percent are not readily attributed to these factors and should be chalked up to changes that are a result of analyst activity in response to a time or a stock-specific event.

The factors that tend to cause analysts to change their earnings estimates are:

1. **Changes in a stock's price:** There is some evidence that a stock's price will go up prior to an analyst revising their earnings estimates. A good explanation for this phenomenon is that due to some fundamental change in a stock's earnings prospects, the stock's price will go up. The analyst, only after

digesting the news of the fundamental change, revises his earnings estimates. Effectively the market is quicker than the analyst in reacting to fundamental changes in a company's earnings prospects. As a result, stock prices beat analysts to the draw. Stock price movement probably explains roughly 11 percent of all earnings estimate revisions.

2. **Earnings Announcements:** As you would expect, analysts revise their earnings estimates in response to earnings announcements. Effectively, the analyst analyzes the earnings report and concludes that his estimates for what the company is going to be earning next quarter are either too low or too high. The analyst essentially processes the information in the earnings report, changes his view about future earnings, and alters his earnings estimates accordingly. Roughly 13 percent of all earnings estimate revisions can be attributed to earnings announcements.

3. **Earnings estimate revisions of other analysts:** The biggest explanation of an individual analyst's future earnings estimate revisions comes from current changes in other analysts' revisions. This is consistent with an analyst revising his earnings estimates because of common information as well as the group-think phenomenon known as *herding*. Roughly 15 percent of all earnings estimate revisions can

be attributed to revisions made by other analysts. Herding seems to be the biggest explanation for earnings estimate revisions.

The best explanation of why other analysts' earnings estimates influence an analyst has to do with how the analyst behaves under uncertainty. As we will see in the chapter on earnings surprises, it is relatively difficult to predict corporate earnings. The consensus earnings estimate consisting of the average forecasts of the analysts following a given stock is only slightly better in predicting earnings than simple trend line extension of historical earnings. Under such uncertainty, an analyst must publicly make an earnings estimate. The analyst must signal to the market that he is an expert about the earnings of the companies that he covers. The problem is that it is like being an expert on the Bears—living, breathing, and eating football does not guarantee that you can predict the score of the game, although it's a good place to start.

The analyst as a result is afraid to be wrong. The analyst wants to be an expert but he is always trying to predict something that has a large random component. As a result, the analyst wants to change his earnings estimates incrementally over time. Nothing says "I do not have a good handle on the earnings prospects of IBM" more than large and frequent changes to earnings estimates. If an analyst believes IBM's earnings are going to be higher than what he previously thought, the analyst, instead of making a bold earnings estimate revision, will make an incremental change and look for confirmation of his beliefs in the earnings estimate revisions from other analysts.

As a result, estimate revisions tend to creep up. This analyst creep or herding helps explain why companies that have received upward earnings estimate revisions are likely to receive them in the future. Basically, the analyst makes his estimate revisions incrementally, because under uncertainty he wants the confirmation of the other analysts following the stock.

4. **Deviation from the consensus:** The difference between an analyst's old earnings estimate and the current consensus is another determinant of an earnings estimate revision. If an analyst's old earnings estimate is significantly above the consensus, the analyst is likely to revise his next earnings estimate downward. Similarly, if an analyst's old earnings estimate is below the consensus, he is likely to revise his earnings estimate upward.

Approximately 12 percent of all earnings estimate revisions can be explained by an analyst seeking the warm, comfy embrace of the consensus. Much like penguins, there is protection from predators in the analyst herd. In order to understand why the analyst is drawn towards the consensus earnings estimate you have to realize what motivates an analyst is being able to generate prestige in the market place. He wants his research report to be the most important research produced on a stock that he is following. The more important an analyst's opinion is viewed by the market, the more his views are listened to, the greater influence he exerts over stock prices, and the more valuable he is to the brokerage firm that employs him.

We know the analyst is basically trying to accomplish feats such as predict stock price movement or corporate earnings that are fraught with uncertainty. In trying to generate perceived expertise under massive uncertainty, the analyst mimics what other analysts are saying. At the end of the day, if an analyst's earnings estimates are wrong and he is different from the consensus, his perceived expertise is hurt. If, however, the analyst is wrong in his earnings estimates but he has the company of other analysts, he is probably not going to receive any negative feedback. The quickest way for an analyst to lose his standing is to make bold earnings estimates that are vastly different from the consensus and completely wrong. Conversely, if an analyst is wrong but he is in agreement with all the other analysts following the stock, his reputation, while likely not enhanced, is not diminished. As a result an analyst craves the safety of the consensus.

5. **Unexpected management guidance:** Occasionally, the corporate managers of the company being followed by the analysts will make an announcement and provide guidance to the marketplace with regards to future earnings. These announcements are relatively rare when compared with the sheer volume of earnings estimate revisions. As a result, only roughly 3 percent of all earnings estimate revisions are attributable to management guidance.

The data regarding the forces generating earnings estimate revisions shows that while earnings are very hard to predict, analyst activity is somewhat predictable (see Exhibit 3.1). The predictable nature of analyst activity is likely due to how the analysts behave under uncertainty. This behavior results in the serial correlation over time of

**Exhibit 3.1   Tale of the Earnings Estimate Revision Tape**

| Source of Earnings Estimate Revision | Percent of Revisions Explained |
| --- | --- |
| Stock Price Movement | 11% |
| Earnings Announcements | 13% |
| Estimate Revisions of Other Analysts | 15% |
| Deviation from the Consensus | 12% |
| Management Guidance | 3% |
| Company Specific Issue | 46% |

earnings estimate revisions. In my mind, the underreaction of the market due to earnings estimate revisions is due to the market not incorporating the fact that once earnings estimates begin to rise, further future upward earnings estimate revisions are likely to materialize.

Several studies have examined earnings estimate revisions in international markets, and most find that international markets also tend to underreact to estimate revisions. Trading on earnings estimate revisions tends to be most profitable in the Netherlands, the United Kingdom, and Germany. France also seems to show excess returns in response to buying stocks receiving upward earnings estimate revisions. Canada has also shown positive results to earnings estimate revision strategies. Japan and Switzerland tend to exhibit weaker results than other countries.

It definitely appears that the stock market tends to underreact to earnings estimate revisions. As a result, if you purchase stocks that have received upward earnings estimate revisions you can generate excess returns above the market. Larger earnings estimate revisions are better, but transaction costs can definitely reduce effective returns. The reason earnings estimate revisions can generate excess returns probably has to do with the way analysts behave under uncertainty. Additionally, earnings estimate revisions also likely benefit from the need of investors to find confirmation of new information, as well as potentially some institutional delay in processing earnings information.

# Chapter Four

# The Big Mo

*A Rolling Stone Ends Up Wealthy*

IF YOU THOUGHT THE "BIG MO" REFERRED TO THE GIRTH of one of the Three Stooges, you'd be wrong. Here we're talking about *momentum*. In equity investing, momentum is the tendency of a stock whose price is rising to keep rising, and a stock whose price is falling to keep falling. It can be boiled down to realizing that the trend really is your friend.

Let's begin by discussing the two different types of investors: fundamental and technical. These are fancy names for the extent to which an investor examines a historical price chart before buying or selling a stock.

---

**In equity investing, momentum is the tendency of a stock whose price is rising to keep rising, and a stock whose price is falling to keep falling. It can be boiled down to realizing that the trend really is your friend.**

---

A fundamental investor focuses on the metrics of the company in question: whether sales are growing and by how much; whether the product being sold is in demand; and whether the company has a sustainable competitive advantage relative to other firms. To the fundamental investor, earnings, valuations, and strategic decisions by the company's management make a difference.

On the other hand, a technical investor generally believes that all the fundamental information concerning a company is already reflected in the company's stock price. These investors look to the historical price movement of the company's stock to see where the stock will go next. To the technician, the market is like a game of blackjack, where the dealt cards play a part in determining which cards will come next. Most investors, with the exception of those who are considered purely quantitative—investors who make their stock trading decisions using a computer that analyzes fundamental data—will look at a chart before buying a stock.

When investment bankers recommend an acquisition to a board of directors, they will almost always show a chart of the target stock. And when an individual investor goes to purchase a stock, he will probably pull up a price chart online. Mutual fund managers do this too, when they look up stock charts before making a purchase decision.

With everyone looking at charts while making decisions on whether to buy or sell stocks, it is not unreasonable to assume that certain chart patterns give rise to certain future price returns. Unfortunately, trying to figure out which chart pattern has value is like trying to find a needle in a haystack. There is an almost unlimited supply of technical trading strategies and testing them all would not provide you with any information as some would look good just by chance. The other main problem in testing technical strategies is that the signals generated are often highly dependent on who is looking at the chart pattern. There tends to be no agreement among technical analysts as to what constitutes a signal: One analyst may see a head and shoulders pattern, but fail to consider the trend at the neckline or the volume; another analyst may see this as an indication for a breakout or a clear signal to sell.

## The Return of Technical Analysis

Technical analysis dates back to the end of the nineteenth century and the work of Charles Dow who, as the founder and editor of the *Wall Street Journal*, first suggested in a series of articles that one could use the rails and industrials averages to assist in identifying trends. The concept grew pretty rapidly after that, and by the late 1960s technical analysis had become an accepted practice.

Technical analysis was rendered a serious setback in 1970 with the growing belief in the efficient market hypothesis. There was a movement among researchers saying that the market was weakly efficient and that there were no patterns in past prices that could be used to predict future prices. By the early 1980s, most brokerage firms' technical research department consisted of a lone analyst—who was seen by most as some sort of witch doctor. This witch doctor would produce reports with drawings scrawled on charts to a dwindling pool of crotchety old investors who continued to employ charting strategies. Well, it now turns out that the crotchety old guys looking at moving averages may not have been so nuts after all.

Up until about 10 years ago the conventional wisdom among researchers was that all technical analysis was pretty much worthless. One professor at Yale showed a team of technical analysts a whole sequence of historical price charts. The technical analysts came up with a multitude of recommendations which they felt very confident about, based on price patterns that they found.

The problem was that the charts were constructed by a computer using a random process that modeled the returns of the stock market. Each tick of price movement was completely independent and random in relation to what had happened previously—there was no pattern, no information in the computer-generated stock charts. Yet the technical analysts found all sorts of patterns embedded in the randomness. The researchers saw this result as a clear indication that people have an uncanny ability to find patterns in truly random data. Kind of like finding shapes in clouds.

The conventional reasoning was that market movements are independent over time. What happens next is not determined by what happened before. To understand this, let's play roulette.

Each realization of the roulette wheel is an independent event. The fact that black came up the last 10 times has no bearing on whether black, red, or green comes up in the next spin of the roulette wheel. The same could be said of a coin toss. If you flip a coin five times and get heads each time, the chance of getting heads on the next toss is still 50-50. Yet people who study the pattern of historical roulette wins find a pattern that they believe gives them a chance to determine what will happen next at the table.

Momentum strategies are based on the belief that some correlation exists between historical price movement and future price movement, but such a statement is almost heretical to those who believe in the efficiency of the stock market. So the question then becomes: If there is a degree of relation between historical stock prices and future stock prices, what risk is an investor incurring by buying those stocks whose future price movement is supposed to be positive?

## Using Momentum-Based Strategies

In a stunning illustration of what can be called a basic problem in economic analysis, what was old is now new again. Current research tends to focus on terms like positive and negative autocorrelation, as opposed to head-and-shoulder patterns, or breakout strategies. While the terms may be statistical in nature, the results are pretty astounding. Based upon a paper written about a decade ago, it appears that looking at past stock movements does have some predictive ability as to what may happen in the future. Perhaps all that was needed was for someone to translate charting intuition into testable criteria.

The data shows two patterns that seem relatively stable, or about as stable as financial data ever becomes. These two patterns are short-term momentum and long-term reversals. In the short-to-medium term, roughly about a calendar quarter or two, stocks that have gone up in price substantially tend to continue to trend upward. However, over the long term, stocks that performed extraordinarily well over the last few years tend to become losers over the next three to five years.

So it seems you can make money by buying momentum in the short term and avoiding momentum in the long term. It is this dance of the short term becoming the long term that contributes to the risk of momentum strategies. Maybe some event will occur that causes the investors with short-term time horizons to suddenly focus on the long term. Thus, the key to price-momentum-based strategies is to get in, but to make sure you don't overstay your welcome.

---

 

**You can make money by buying momentum in the short term and avoiding momentum in the long term. It is this dance of the short term becoming the long term that contributes to the risk of momentum strategies.**

---

One interesting way to examine the effectiveness of momentum based strategies is to create hedged portfolios and see what returns they generate. A hedged portfolio consists of going long a basket of stocks and short an equal dollar amount in another basket of stocks. Shorting a stock effectively means you borrow shares from a broker and then sell the shares in the market. If you are short a portfolio of stocks you effectively profit if the portfolio falls in value. Hedged portfolios constructed based on price momentum have historically returned around 12 percent annually gross of all transaction costs.

The long and short sides of the hedged portfolio are generated by sorting a universe of companies into deciles based on their historical price momentum. Effectively, the hedged portfolio is long a basket of stocks with high price momentum and short a basket of stocks with low price momentum.

If there were no momentum effects you would expect roughly zero returns from the hedged portfolio. Instead, we find returns that average roughly one percent per month.

These hedged return studies tend to show that the top decile portfolio (the set of stocks that were the best performers over the recent past—those stocks that generated the highest level of returns in the past) tends to continue to outperform, and the bottom decile (the set of stocks that were the worst performers over the recent past) continues to lose.

The optimal strategy would thus appear to take a long position on stocks which have been performing well and a short position on stocks which have been performing poorly. This strategy would theoretically produce positive returns over the long haul. This is really a phenomenal result. By creating a portfolio with practically no market or beta risk—as the portfolio is dollar neutral—positive returns can be generated over time. Interestingly enough, the returns generated by this momentum-based hedged strategy continue to be statistically positive even after controlling for risk.

This short-term momentum strategy looked quite promising overall until the turn of the century. Around the year 2000, momentum-based strategies took quite a beating, giving up in the period of a few years their gains over the past decade. However, after five years, the normal relationship was reestablished, and high momentum stocks began outperforming low momentum stocks again.

It looks like for short-term momentum-based strategies the best results can be obtained using what is called a 12/3 split. What this means is sorting the universe of stocks into deciles based upon how they performed over the past year, and then holding the portfolio for the next three months. It also looks like performance can slightly be increased if you lag the construction period by one week. What this means is that you sort the stocks into deciles, but base the sorting on the yearly returns of the stock as of one week ago.

Another appealing strategy is a 6/6 split. A 2001 study on market momentum sorted stocks into winner and loser portfolios that consisted of the best and worst performing deciles (the top and bottom 10 percent), respectively, based upon their returns over the past six months. Upon examining the subsequent performance of these two portfolios over a six-month holding period, the top decile portfolio outperformed the bottom decile portfolio by 1.39 percent per month over the six-month holding period. As in previous studies, the majority of the outperformance was due to the continued performance of the winner portfolio. Momentum clearly seems to work better on the long side than on the short side.

Similar results can be obtained by buying stocks that trade near their 52-week highs and using traditional moving averages. In a moving-average strategy, you buy stocks whose prices are substantially above the average stock price over the past 120 or 240 days. In fact, some research shows that moving-average strategies actually outperform the traditional decile sorting methodology. It also looks like buying stocks near their 52-week highs is a slightly better predictor of returns than sorting stocks into the 6/6 split.

Although in the short term high momentum stocks tend to generate excess returns, over longer holding periods the effect is reversed. The trend may be your friend when trading a 12/3 or 6/6 momentum strategy, but when holding stocks for longer periods the trend is more of a frenemy.

A 36/36 split strategy in which stocks are sorted into deciles based on their return over the past 36 months and then held for the next 36 months, generates very interesting results. When the holding and creation period is extended, what you find is that the high momentum stocks substantially underperform the low momentum stocks. If you are looking to hold stocks for multiple years, it is the multiyear negative momentum portfolios or losers you want to own. The winners over the past few years actually underperform over the next few years.

Thus it appears that momentum works over the short term, but over the long term a reversal pattern tends to take hold. The long-term reversal pattern is explained to some extent by reversion to the mean over long periods of time.

The same statistical effect that causes two very tall adults to have children that are likely to be shorter than they are may also explain the long-term reversal momentum strategy.

Potentially, if a stock's price grows by too great an amount over a long period of time, then the stock is due statistically for a period of weak performance. Such a result is a clear violation of the independence of stock returns.

It shows the market behaving less like a roulette wheel and more like a deck of cards in which high face cards have all been dealt, making the player due for a series of lower value cards. This may occur, however, if a stock's long-term rate of return is capped. While any stock may be able to generate a 100 percent annualized rate of return for a few years running, the stock is due for a breather at some point, perhaps due to increased competition from other companies. Apple can only sell so many iPads before competitors decide to enter the fray.

## When the Strategy Works Best

What is somewhat unusual is that momentum seems to work better for mid-cap stocks than for either large- or small-cap stocks. A study about 10 years ago evaluated a 6/6 momentum strategy where the winner and loser portfolios are characterized as the best and worst performing 30th percentiles, respectively. Using data from January 1980 to December 1996, the study cleverly performs what is effectively a double sort within the winner and loser portfolios. Both the winner and losing portfolios are splice according to mark capitalization into deciles. In this way you can examine if price momentum effects are greater among large-cap or small-cap stocks. The results are very interesting and it looks like there may be an inverted U-shaped pattern to momentum returns across market-capitalization deciles. Momentum returns for these (30 percent) long-short momentum portfolios appeared to be nonexistent for the smallest and largest stocks but significantly positive for medium-sized stocks.

Financial data analysis is rarely conclusive and although the double sorting research shows momentum is strongest among mid-cap stocks other research indicates that price-momentum-based strategies are statistically stronger for stocks with lower analyst coverage. As one progresses from low to high analyst coverage, price-momentum profits tend to shrink. This result suggests that momentum-based returns may be driven by the proprietary nature of early information flow. Effectively, momentum strategies may work better the fewer people cover or are familiar with a stock. The information regarding the fundamental prospects of the company are disseminated slowly and as a result price momentum generates good returns.

In other words, the more people who know about an attractive stock, the more efficient the market is regarding the stock, and the less likely price momentum will generate excess returns.

What is very encouraging about momentum-based strategies is that they seem to work across most international markets. A study at momentum strategies in 39 different non-U.S. equity markets, finding significant evidence of large momentum profits in most markets; interestingly, the

study found that momentum profits are not highly correlated across these markets. This seems to be an indication
that macroeconomic factors are probably not driving
momentum returns. Emerging markets also exhibit signs
of momentum. All of this evidence points potentially to a
behavioral explanation for the momentum anomaly.

In both the short-term and long-term momentum cases,
the momentum profits seem to hold for raw returns as well
as for risk-adjusted returns. This means that momentum-
based strategies, similar to value-based strategies, appear
to deliver excess returns without excess risks. In order for
there not to be a free lunch, the extra returns you earn by
following a momentum-based strategy must be associated
with extra risk. The key question is: What is the risk borne
by holding high-momentum stocks?

Like the other strategies discussed in this book, maybe
the higher returns are compensation for an unknown
higher level of risk associated with momentum portfolios.
I tend to believe the best explanation for the returns of
momentum-based strategies lies in the realm of investor
behavior. The key to explaining momentum strategies lies
not within the stars but within ourselves.

## An Individual Problem

Individual investors seem to suffer from a problem that
institutional investors do not incur. They tend to hold

losing stocks too long and sell winning stocks too soon. It is very possible that this behavior might explain the momentum phenomenon.

Investors typically do not treat gains and losses the same. For most people the pain of regret exceeds the joy of pride. People generally feel twice as much pain from losing $100 than the happiness they feel from making $100. This sort of asymmetric treatment of gains and losses may play a role in the timing decisions of investors. As a result, investors may underreact to positive new information and be slow to sell stocks on negative information.

An interesting study examines actual transaction data from January 1983 to December 2002. What the study basically shows is that small traders tend to engage in trades that would contribute to momentum returns, such as under reacting to losses and selling gains too early. Large institutional investors however seem to react more accurately to gains and losses. By examining buying and selling pressures for both momentum winners and losers, the study showed that small investors tend to react slower to price movement, whether positive or negative, than large or institutional traders. This may be due to such factors as uncertainty about validity of information on the stock, emotional bias, past performance of the stock or even peer pressure—but it definitely showed that momentum strategies are influenced by investor bias. That is, stocks that have greater ownership by individuals tend to show stronger momentum profits.

If it were the case that individuals contribute to momentum returns by behavioral biases we would expect to see stocks with low volume—which would be more likely to be held by individuals—to exhibit stronger momentum returns. This is exactly what researchers find is the case, and a stock's past trading volume is a good predictor of how strong the momentum effect is and the extent to which the momentum effect persists. Momentum strategies seem to work better among stocks with low volume—the same types of stocks that are either neglected by institutions or, alternatively, held by individuals.

There is also strong evidence to suggest that it is the small, individual investors who are, in aggregate, driving momentum. Thus, when implementing momentum-based strategies, it makes sense to focus on the universe of stocks that is traded primarily by individual investors as opposed to institutional investors. You can determine this by examining the percentage of institutional holdings, looking for low volume, or, alternatively, looking for low analyst coverage. All these characteristics should contribute to stronger momentum returns.

Another possible explanation for the persistence of momentum-based returns is that the momentum reflects something that is real in the economy. For instance, the momentum could potentially reflect broad-based economic strength in the economy. This can be tested by examining whether momentum-based returns can be explained by variables that describe the macroeconomic conditions.

When you examine how momentum is effected by macroeconomic conditions you find an intriguing result. Over the past seventy years, it looks like momentum based strategies only generate excess returns in periods of economic expansion. Even more interesting, momentum returns turn negative during a recession. While the results are interesting they must be taken with a grain of salt as the business cycle dating process is more of an art than a science. Nevertheless, it looks like momentum strategies do not work well in a recession. In fact in a recession the low momentum stocks actually seem to outperform the high momentum stocks over the next three months.

―――――――――――― ∾ ――――――――――――

**In order to make the trend your friend, the key is to look for short-term momentum. This is not a great strategy to employ before going into a recession—but if you could predict when the recessions would hit, you could make a fortune going on the road as a fortune teller.**

So, in order to make the trend your friend, the key is to look for short-term momentum. This is not a great strategy to employ before going into a recession—but if you could predict when the recessions would hit, you could make a fortune going on the road as a fortune teller.

Additionally, when implementing momentum-based strategies, it makes sense to focus on a universe of stocks that is traded primarily by individual investors as opposed to institutional investors. Look for mid-cap stocks and hold the portfolio for about a quarter. Use the 52-week high or a moving average to select your stocks and try to focus on companies that are traded primarily by individuals. Just be careful of the momentum reversals in which the progress of several years can be wiped out over a few months.

# The Inside Story

~

## *Why Buying a Stock Is Like Going to the Used-Car Lot*

IN SOME WAYS BUYING PUBLICLY TRADED EQUITY IS A LOT like purchasing a used car. When you buy a used car the seller knows a lot more about the car than you do. The seller knows if the car is a "lemon"—a poorly working car that has been spiffed up in order to sell. A similar issue exists when purchasing stocks. But instead of the car salesman or former owner, the people who truly know the value of the company are its executives and the investors with the most stock in the company. These people will have far more information about the value of the stock than the average individual equity buyer.

One interesting investment strategy attempts to piggyback on the trading decisions made by these informed individuals, also known as insiders. Who are we calling insiders? Insiders are considered to be anyone with access to information related to the business and financial workings of a company. This would include, of course, members of the board of directors, the officers, and other high-level employees. Consultants and lawyers working for the corporate officers also qualify as insiders as do shareholders that hold a large chunk of the company's stock.

Now, if these people want to trade in the stock of a company for which they are an insider they are allowed if they are not trading on nonpublic material information and they publicly report their transactions. For instance, if the CEO of a company knew the company was going to be acquired because he was the one involved in the acquisition talks, that CEO would not be able to purchase shares in anticipation of the acquisition. However, if the CEO simply thought his company's shares were undervalued but there was not any acquisition pending, the CEO could purchase the shares of his company in the open market. All the CEO has to do in this case is report his transactions publicly during a certain time period after making the transaction.

As an individual, the best investment strategy is to be the insider—become the CEO of a publicly traded company and make a good living on stock options. Unfortunately, for most investors, this is not a possibility and a reasonable alternative is to piggyback on the publicly disclosed trading activity of the insiders. This essentially means that when the CEO of a company buys the shares of his company, you should too—the reason being that the CEO of the company is probably in a better position than an average stock investor to evaluate the prospects of his company and determine whether his company's stock is undervalued. It is probably a good rule of thumb that if the insiders of a company are buying, you should be buying as well, and if the insiders are selling, you should probably be avoiding the stock.

Various studies have shown that investment strategies focused on the publicly disclosed insider data have generated returns in excess of the market over the past four decades. A debate exists as to whether the excess returns generated by this strategy are simply the result of information asymmetry—that is, the insiders are better informed than the rest of the market—or whether the excess returns result from specific information leaking out through the insiders. One study that shows some degree of information leakage examines 3700 takeover targets over the last 20 years. As expected, the rate of insider purchases of their company's stock fell in the six-month period prior to the announcement of the acquisition of the company. However, it looks like sales fell off at a greater rate. This effectively shows that insiders may have profited from the upcoming acquisition by refraining from selling shares. In any case, insiders should be seen as informed agents and as a result it makes sense to pay attention to their trading activity.

## The More Things Change . . .

Before 2002, insiders had anywhere between 10 and 40 days to publicly report their transactions. This meant if the CEO bought the shares of his company he would have to publicly file this information within 40 days. However, it was not uncommon for the transaction to be reported even later, since the whole process was driven by the actual filing of physical papers. Today, however, following the Sarbanes-Oxley Act of 2002 (which introduced major changes to the regulation of financial practice and corporate governance), insiders must report transactions involving their own company's shares within two days. Transactions are filed electronically and are publicly available via the Internet. As a result, it is now possible for an average investor to more easily piggyback on the insider trades.

There is a possibility, however, that the changes in the disclosure rules may have impacted the way the insiders trade, and thus the return patterns of an insider trading strategy may have significantly changed. We just can't tell until enough time has passed so that returns can accurately be compared.

If you examine the returns made by the insiders themselves you find that, based upon the date of the trade, as opposed to the date of disclosure, insiders make significant excess returns. A fairly recent study shows that insiders earned about 6 percent above the return generated by similar types of stocks in the six months following the actual purchases made by the insiders. Roughly one-third of this excess return seemed to occur in the first month following the date of the actual insider purchase. This excess return can be generated by imitating the insider purchases made and giving each transaction a weight proportional to the amount of money the insider spent on the purchase. The major issue is that these returns are based upon the date of the insider trade as opposed to the date of the disclosure of the trade. Nevertheless, the returns indicate that insiders posses information that helps them generate excess returns.

As many other studies have also shown, this study indicates that insider buying seems to have stronger predictive ability than insider selling. This is understandable, for there are many reasons why an insider may sell a stock—to diversify wealth or to make a big purchase like a house, for example. However, there is only one good reason for the insider to purchase shares: He thinks the price of the stock is going up. Thus, it appears that insider trading is more effective in determining which shares to buy than in identifying which shares to sell.

It also seems to be the case that different types of insiders have different levels of predictive ability regarding their returns. It looks like officer-directors—individuals who are directors as well as officers of the company—tend to have the highest abnormal returns on their trading, while individuals who are simply officers of the company tend to have the lowest level of abnormal returns. Large 10 percent owners also seem to generate higher abnormal returns around their trading than do pure officers.

Returns are also increased when some form of intensity measurement is employed. What this effectively means is that although one individual insider may be wrong in terms of his conviction to buy or sell, when multiple insiders are buying around the same time it may provide a stronger signal to the marketplace. If you focus on piggybacking on the purchases made by at least three insiders over a three-month period, the average monthly return you can generate over the past 27 years is a hair under 2 percent per month, while the S&P 500 has generated a little more than 1 percent per month. These return numbers exclude transaction costs.

It is important to realize though that these returns are average monthly returns. As the old saying goes, it is possible to drown in a lake where the average water height is only one foot. The biggest problem with an insider trading strategy is that the returns are not consistent year after year. As a result, an investor using insider activity as a basis for selecting securities must have a long enough time frame in order to wait out the bad years and participate in the good years.

## It Depends on the Company

It also looks like insider trading tends to work better in cases where there is a greater degree of information asymmetry. For instance, one would not think that insider buying would work particularly well for companies whose earnings are primarily driven by large macro economic factors. If the directors of Exxon bought a substantial amount of XOM stock, this would not necessarily translate into any significant movement in the share price. However, for firms such as biotechnology companies where specific product information is very important in determining earnings, one would expect insider trading to be substantially more effective. For the most part this is what we see: The greater the information asymmetry of the industry, the more insider trading seems to work as a strategy.

Generally speaking, insider buying seems to be most predictive in the transportation, consumer staples— including drug companies, technology, financial, and business services sectors. Conversely, insider buying is least effective in the capital goods, basic materials, energy, consumer cyclical, and utilities sectors.

We also see that insider trading seems to work better with small-cap companies than with large-cap companies. Part of this may be because, in a small-cap company, when an insider buys shares of his company he actually may work harder to improve his company's performance. With a large company, this motivation factor may be more subdued, since any one individual's ability to influence a company's stock price is lessened the larger the organization becomes.

It is also very likely that small-cap companies exhibit a greater degree of information asymmetry. For Microsoft there is not much that Steve Balmer or Bill Gates knows about the company's prospects that is not already known by analysts or astute investors. Quite simply, Microsoft is so large that the company's prospects are widely known. The prospects of a small-cap technology company are for the most part unknown by the market, and as a result the insider trading of the small-cap technology company has a significantly greater signaling effect on the market. The data seems to back this up, and small-cap stocks experiencing intensive insider buying seem to outperform the S&P 500 by almost 0.91 percent per month gross of all transaction costs.

## Why Insiders Buy and Sell

For the most part, insider selling is not particularly useful. As stock-option-based compensation has become much more widespread, most corporate officers tend to sell more stock for liquidity purposes and to build a more diverse portfolio. However, there are some times when insider selling tends to be relatively useful.

About 10 years ago, insiders were allowed to set up a selling rule that enables insiders to sell shares using a written algorithm—for instance, selling a certain number of shares each and every month for the next few years regardless of fluctuation in a stock's price. It appears that following the implementation of such a strategy a company's stock will underperform the market by around 2 percent over the next six months.

A more interesting phenomenon seems to occur when insiders sell their shares and use the proceeds to buy a new house. A somewhat voyeristic 2007 study indicated that the purchase of a large luxury home by a company CEO almost always preceded negative performance of the company's stock.

Generally speaking, if insiders are buying someone must be selling them shares. For the most part insiders tend to trade more like individuals than institutions. Institutions tend to trade in the opposite direction of the insiders. This result is largely because the insider transactions tend to be more contrarian in nature, and institutions in aggregate tend to be slightly more momentum-focused in their trading. However, it is very clear, based upon institutional investors' use of insider transaction data, that many institutions tend to implement insider-trading-based strategies. The insider trading strategies seem to be more employed by institutions focused on smaller cap companies.

---

**Insiders tend to trade more like individuals than institutions. Institutions tend to trade in the opposite direction of the insiders. This result is largely because the insider transactions tend to be more contrarian in nature, and institutions in aggregate tend to be slightly more momentum-focused in their trading.**

---

One big factor in considering implementing insider trading-based strategies has to do with the time delay between the insider's trade, the dissemination of the trade, and the subjective decision to act upon the information. Several newsletters based on insider trading seem to have generated sub-par results over the same time periods in which an intensive insider buying strategy appeared to work. This seems to point out that acting quickly and decisively on insider trading data seems to be key in generating returns.

Insiders are definitely contrarians. Insiders tend to buy when prices are declining and sell when prices are rising. This is the opposite of a momentum investor, and as a result insider-based strategies should bear lower than normal correlation to momentum-based strategies. It is important to remember, though, that insider trading appears to occur more frequently in smaller companies or those that are in a distressed condition. As a result, a strategy that focuses on multiple insiders buying may unduly lead to small-cap stocks with high growth prospects or to stocks of companies that are under distress.

When you combine insider trading with analyst recommendations, you can reach some interesting results.

When insiders are net sellers, analyst downgrades don't seem to lead to unusual returns. This seems to indicate that when analysts agree with insiders that a company's stock price should fall, the analysts are usually the last people to know and the information is already baked into the stock price. Analyst downgrades seem to generate abnormal negative returns only when there is no insider selling.

## A Global Gem

What is encouraging about insider trading, like several of the other strategies considered in this book, is that it appears to be profitable in countries other than the United States. It looks like piggybacking on insiders can be employed profitably in Europe and some Asian markets as well. Research shows that insider trading strategies are effective in Germany and work particularly well in the Netherlands. Positive results are also found in the United Kingdom, Spain, Italy, Hong Kong, and Poland. In some of these countries the delay between when the outsider mimics the insider transaction causes what appears to be profitable strategies to lose their effectiveness. In Spain, for instance, securities regulations require a 39-day delay between the insider transaction and its announcement. As a result, outsiders mimicking insider trades do not earn excess returns. In most of these international studies, the abnormal returns seem to be concentrated in the smaller companies just as they are in the United States. This seems to point to information asymmetry as a source of the excess returns due to mimicking insider activity.

The biggest issue with insider trading strategies is whether an outsider receives the insider trading data quickly enough to make a profit. Harvard business professor Francois Brochet tackled this question in a 2010 study of insider transactions occuring between 1997 and 2006. Before the Sarbanes-Oxley Act, when the delay from an insider engaging in a purchase and that information being filed publicly could be between 10 and 40 days, the average three-day cumulative excess return over the market from the day the information was filed was about 0.6 percent. What this means is that from the day the insider trading purchase was actually filed the stocks that were purchased outperformed the market by about 0.6 percent over the next three days.

After the Sarbanes-Oxley Act, which requires the insider to file his purchase within two days, the cumulative excess more than tripled to 1.9 percent. What this implies is that Sarbanes-Oxley may have made piggybacking on insider purchases a more profitable strategy by substantially reducing the time delay between the insider purchase and the disclosure to the market. Nevertheless, this data examines insider buying from the date of filing, and there are often additional delays between the filing and the insider purchase information actually being acted upon by investors.

## Say It Ain't So, Joe

The consistency of insider trading is a bit of an issue. The data show that there can be multiple years in which an

insider trading strategy employing some degree of intensity measurement underperforms the market. Thus, like
many of the other strategies examined, it is hard to predict
when the excess returns due to piggybacking on insiders
will in fact materialize. It takes a tremendous amount of
patience for an investor to remain committed to an investment strategy after three years of underperformance, but
that appears to be necessary to realize the excess returns
of the strategy. This may also explain why the insider
trading anomaly tends to persist many years after first
being discovered, and why there is no large institutional
embracing of the strategy.

It seems that, based on the data, the market responds
to insider buying mostly within the first 30 days of the
insider purchase. Then there seems to be additional excess
returns over the market starting roughly six months following the initial purchase. The excess returns seem to be
very time dependent, and there is a benefit to acting
quickly in response to insider buying activity. It is possible that, as a result of the need for speed, that small traders and mutual funds can benefit the most from utilizing
insider trading transactions.

What is very clear from the data over the past 40
years is that insiders have some predictive ability in their
timing of purchases of their own stocks. The key is when
the information becomes available to investors. It appears

that advances in information technology are effectively reducing the time period required to file, and they are helping make insider trading a more effective strategy.

In any case, the key to using disclosed insider trading effectively seems to be to implement the strategy on the long side as opposed to the short side. Insider buying for the most part is far more effective than insider selling. Instead of looking for a buy signal from just one insider, an investor should focus on insider buying from multiple insiders over a given time frame. Insider buying by officers who also serve as directors looks like it is a slightly more powerful signal than insider buying from a regular officer who does not serve as a director.

Insider buying seems to be more effective in generating excess returns among smaller cap companies and companies that are under distress. These types of companies tend to be highly volatile, and the excess returns from insider buying do not seem to be consistent over time. All of this points to insider buying as being a complementary strategy to a core strategy. An investor needs a high amount of confidence in insider buying to stick to the strategy through its volatility and periods of poor performance.

Finally, it is very important to get the insider trading data and act upon the data as quickly as possible. The fact that an insider purchased shares more than five or six months ago has little predictive ability to what will happen to the stock

---

**The strategy of piggybacking on insider purchases is not for everyone. But, when combined with other strategies discussed in this book, insider buying should help generate additional excess returns.**

---

price next. If the insider purchased shares a few days ago, the majority of the excess returns seem to take place within the first 30 days of the insider making the trade. The quicker the insider purchase is filed, and the quicker an investor acts upon the filing, the better returns the insider buying will generate for the outsider. The strategy of piggybacking on insider purchases is not for everyone. But, when combined with other strategies discussed in this book, insider buying should help generate additional excess returns.

*Chapter Six*

# Song of the Shares

~

*Why You Want to Listen to
Groucho Marx*

GROUCHO MARX ONCE SAID THAT HE NEVER WANTED TO be a member of a club that would have him as a member. Nowhere is this quote more applicable than in the equity markets. At the end of the day, after all the fundamental analysis and hype, the fact remains that the only IPOs—initial public offerings—you want to buy are those that you have trouble getting access to. The IPOs that are actually offered to you are the ones you want to take a pass on. That being said, there is growing evidence that, by following various signals sent by management during financing activities, excess returns can be generated.

There appear to be negative excess returns generated following an IPO, as well as positive excess returns that can be generated by following share repurchases, dividend increases, and certain financing announcements. These patterns represent anomalies, since they are empirical results that seem to be inconsistent with an efficient market. As we'll see, if a company wants to sell you stock, take a pass. And if a company wants to buy stock from you, the best course of action is not to sell.

In an initial public offering a private company sells its shares for the first time on the open market. In doing so the company transforms itself from a business with a limited shareholder base into a publicly traded corporation where anyone can purchase shares on the open market. While the outliers often get the most attention, the Googles of the world are the exception rather than the rule.

In theory, companies should go public when their growth prospects are such that they require capital in excess of what can be obtained through bank financing or other private means. Think of a technology company growing so fast that it eats cash at a fast rate and cash is not available from the usual sources of funds for growth, such as private equity investments. The theory is that there is not enough cash available from banks to finance growth, and there aren't enough deep-pocketed investors willing to provide the amounts of equity necessary for the build out of the business. The only option for attaining growth is to sell shares to the public.

In practice, however, what really determines whether a company goes public are valuation concerns. In the real world, companies go public because the value the equity markets place on the shares compels the current private shareholders to sell. Companies go public in order to make money for their current shareholders, rather than to provide capital for growth.

---

**Companies go public because the value the equity markets place on the shares compels the current private shareholders to sell. Companies go public in order to make money for their current shareholders, rather than to provide capital for growth.**

---

## A Big, Ugly Investor Trap

In an IPO, or initial public offering, the net result is that private shareholders sell their shares to the public at a price that is far greater than what they feel the company is worth. If you buy the shares by participating in the IPO, then statistically speaking, you will lose money over time. The data bear this out very clearly.

The easiest way to see this result is to look at the returns you would have generated if you purchased IPOs. One study examining more than 1,500 initial public offerings showed that by purchasing the IPOs, an investor would have generated cumulative average returns of minus nearly 30 percent for the 36 months following the IPO. The results clearly indicate that an investor should short a basket of stocks following the IPO rather than participate in the offering process.

Well, you might say that perhaps this underperformance is because IPOs are more likely to be smaller-cap companies in high-growth industries and that over time these smaller-cap stocks underperformed due to their market capitalization and industry concentration. This, however, does not seem to be the case and the results hold even after the returns are matched to similar firms by both size and industry. Effectively, the stocks of companies engaging in IPOs underperform their peers when looked at from a buy-and-hold perspective as well as from a monthly rebalancing perspective.

One explanation for the poor performance from holding IPOs is that investors are buying too much into the hype and are disappointed when the actual fundamental results of the business materialize. The trees never quite grow to the sky, no matter how fast the sapling has sprouted from a seed. Effectively, in aggregate, investors may be too optimistic about a firm's prospects when the firm is in a high-growth industry.

Additional studies looking at more recent data come to the same conclusion—you generally lose money by buying IPOs. Across the board, IPOs are in aggregate overvalued. Based upon peer matching and fundamental analysis, it looks like IPOs were overvalued anywhere in a range from 14 to 50 percent. The basic conclusion is that investors put too much faith in overly optimistic forecasts about the company's potential for growth and overlook or even ignore whether the company is actually profitable, in valuing the IPOs.

It also appears to make a difference whether the primary backers of the publicly traded company are venture capital firms. A study done in the mid 1990s shows that over a five-year period following an offering, non-venture-capital backed IPOs underperformed an equally weighted benchmark by 33 percent cumulatively, while venture-backed IPOs underperformed an equally weighted benchmark by 16 percent. Both IPOs underperformed, but investors were hurt far more buying the IPOs that lacked the venture capital funding. Apparently, a good portion of the documented IPOs' underperformance stemmed from non-venture-backed IPOs, especially among smaller firms.

On average, if a company is selling stock to the public, you don't want to buy. Data very clearly shows that not only do IPOs substantially underperform the market, but companies engaging in secondary equity offerings—in which an already public company issues additional shares in order to raise capital also underperform. It does not seem to matter if the equity is being offered for the first, second, or third time. The stocks of companies issuing shares are more likely to be losers than winners.

## A Chance at Profiting

So if you should generally avoid IPOs—and especially avoid non-venture-funded IPOs—is there any way you can use IPOs to try to generate excess returns? The answer, very interestingly, lies with potentially using the aggregate level of IPOs as a means of gauging the market's overall frothiness. Periods when companies are issuing large amounts of equity are generally followed by periods of low overall market returns. Conversely a period consisting of a dearth of IPO activity generally results in a strong equity market for the next half-decade.

This makes a certain amount of sense, since private companies are more likely to go public when there is more demand for publicly traded equities than there is supply.

This supply imbalance occurs primarily when the demand is overheated because of run-ups in stock prices. Another potential explanation is that the pattern is caused by the managers of the private company being able to time their equity issuance to coincide with what they see in real time as market peaks. Companies sell shares only when investors are willing to pay through the nose for them.

Imagine a company looking to finance growth. The managers of the company have the option to finance the growth by issuing either debt or equity. They will likely choose to issue debt if the market value of the debt issued is higher than what the managers think their debt is truly worth. Similarly, the managers will issue equity when they feel that the price paid by the public for the equity they are issuing is greater than what the equity is intrinsically worth. Effectively, managers issue equity when their equity is expensive. This produces an interesting signal: If many companies are issuing equity either through initial public offerings or secondary offerings, it may be an indication the market is overvalued.

Additionally, when the percentage of equity issuance starts to increase dramatically relative to the historical level of debt issuances, it is an indication that the insiders who manage the companies in aggregate see the market as expensive. The time you want to buy stocks is when the managers of the companies don't want to part with their shares. The good news for investors today is that we are likely in such a period, and the dearth of IPOs and secondary equity offerings indicate the market may be heading higher over the next half of a decade.

An important caveat is that the IPO underperformance results are not uniform across studies or sub-samples of firms. Like many of the strategies we have looked at in this book, the IPO results do not hold for all periods. Consequently, there are several periods when IPOs substantially outperform the market. Also the results do not hold for every single company, and the media tend to focus on the winners and ignore the losers. It is relatively easy to fall into a lottery ticket mentality by dreaming of participating in the next Google, but the reality is that on the whole, statistically, IPOs do not make good investments.

When calculating returns, many of the IPO studies assume investors buy the newly issued stock at the price the company is trading at on the end of the first day of trading as opposed to the offer price at which the shares are purchased directly from the underwriter. Investment banks generally price the shares in the prospectus below what they believe the shares will trade at in the market in order to generate interest in the IPO. Thus, the negative excess returns from holding IPOs may be lessened by buying the IPO at the price in the prospectus directly from the investment bank. There is a strategy employed by wealthy investors where they buy IPOs at the offer price and quickly flip the shares in a matter of days for a profit.

However, this is where we come back to the Groucho Marx quote. If an IPO is believed to be successful and will likely result in a large jump above the offer price—effectively the price at which you buy shares directly from the investment bank—to the price it trades at in the market, then the IPO is going to be in very high demand by large institutional investors. If, however, the IPO is believed to potentially be broken and is not likely to trade above its offer price, the IPO will not be in very high demand. As an individual investor, or perhaps even a moderate sized institutional investor, the IPOs you will be offered will be those that are likely to be broken.

~

**Investment banks generally price the shares in the prospectus below what they believe the share will trade at in the market in order to generate interest in the IPO. Thus the negative excess returns from holding IPOs may be lessened by buying the IPO at the price in the prospectus directly from the investment bank.**

If the IPO is believed to be successful, the investment bank will have no problem raising the money and will thus not need to pitch anyone except their most important clients. Unless you are a truly big commission-generating institution for an investment bank, the fact that you are being offered an IPO is a clear indication that the IPO will likely be broken.

## When a Company Buys Its Own Shares

But all is not lost. Sometimes firms do the opposite of issuing shares: They buy back their publicly traded shares in the open market—the same way an investor might buy the company's shares in a brokerage account. There are really three potential reasons a company would buy back its stock. One reason for a buyback is for the company to manage its reported earnings per share. If management is not able to increase the company's earnings, one way management can increase earnings per share is to reduce the number of shares outstanding. Another reason for stock buybacks is to avoid the double taxation of dividends. If a company simply returns cash to shareholders, shareholders must pay taxes on the dividends received. Share buybacks are a means of returning cash to investors without those investors incurring extra taxes. Finally, the most important reason to buy back shares is for management to signal to the market that their shares are undervalued. If you examine the data, it seems to indicate that what drives most share buybacks is undervaluation.

Share buybacks are generally good news for a stock. When a company is buying back its shares it usually is an indication that the company's managers feel their shares are undervalued. The managers reason that the company can make more money by buying its undervalued shares in the open market than by deploying the company's capital in growing the business. While a cynic might argue that this is an indication of a lack of growth prospects in the company's core business, the data clearly show it is more of an indication that the company's stock is attractively valued. Effectively, share buybacks are an indication that the managers of the company see their shares as undervalued. As a general rule of thumb, when a company buys back its shares, you should mimic the company's actions and buy more shares as well.

Some companies go a step further, and instead of buying their shares on the open market they issue what is essentially a self-tender offer. Self-tenders are relatively uncommon when compared to share buybacks but are much more powerful signals. In a self-tender offer, a formal announcement by the company is made to existing holders for them to sell a fixed number of shares back to the company. Following a simple trading strategy around repurchase tender offers, one can generate sky-high abnormal stock returns of more than 9 percent in one week, according to some studies. But it is important to realize that repurchase tender offers rarely occur in today's business environment and the effect really only holds in small-cap firms.

Nevertheless, a portfolio consisting of firms repurchasing their shares through tender offers outperforms the market quite substantially. However, if you look at the larger firms the behavior is significantly different. Large-cap firms tend to experience excess returns prior to the tender-offer announcement, and zero excess returns once the announcement is implemented. The general belief is tender offers by large firms are part of a wide corporate restructuring strategy, while with a small firm the tender offer signals massive undervaluation.

While self-tender offers are few and far between, numerous studies focused on open share buybacks offer very interesting results. In a 1995 study focusing on more than 1,200 open share repurchases during the 1980s, companies buying back their stock usually outperformed the market in the four-year period following the repurchase announcement.

Abnormal stock returns tend to trend in the same direction as the initial stock price reaction, in a manner much like equity issuances; however, open market share repurchases are the opposite of equity issuances and would trend positive, in this case, rather than negative. I attribute this to signaling—the market realizes that management is buying shares because they truly are undervalued.

A follow-up study in 2009 tested whether the excess returns due to share repurchases and tender offers was consistent using a larger sample and data which reflected current market parameters. The initial evaluation showed that the excess returns from buybacks were not specific to a particular time in the market or a particular segment of stocks being traded. This means that investors can generate excess returns by piggybacking on share buybacks. An investor just needs to be careful that the share buybacks are actually occurring and not simply announced. It is not unheard of for a company not to complete announced share buybacks, or to announce share buybacks in an open-ended fashion so that the buyback can be cancelled. In order to profit from share buybacks the company must actually purchase the shares.

The recent studies also seem to indicate that arbitrageurs have not been able to exploit this buyback strategy, and returns can still be generated by following the piggyback strategies highlighted in earlier studies. Examining more than 3,400 open market repurchase programs announced throughout the 1990s some interesting research shows that large, long-run, abnormal returns were still as significant, especially for value stocks, as they had always been. Again, the results seem to be stronger with smaller capitalization stocks.

One novel explanation for the excess returns due to buy backs has to do with analyst behavior. People, and analysts in particular, are often very reluctant to change their mind, especially once they have staked out a position. An analyst who has travelled the country telling investors to avoid a stock is much more likely to become lukewarm on the stock than he is to suddenly issue a buy recommendation. Potentially, a firm's repurchase program is in direct response to a mistake made by financial analysts who follow the firm. The repurchase announcement is a way for the firm's management to tell the market that despite what the analyst is saying, the stock is undervalued. This could explain why buyback results are stronger among smaller-cap stocks as smaller-cap stocks tend to have lower analyst coverage.

If you look closely at the data it seems you can finally put to rest the long debate regarding the reasons managers choose to buy back their firms' stock. The data suggest that the most important reason for share repurchases is exploiting undervaluation. As a result, you can generate excess returns by piggybacking on the announcement of buybacks.

## Dividends and Acquisitions

Generally, you should pay attention when a company announces an acquisition. Companies that perform acquisitions should be avoided. Think of the person at an art auction who wins the item up for bidding. The winner paid more than anyone else offered for a given item, and likely he over-paid. The same is pretty much true in an acquisition—the winner in a competitive auction almost always overpays.

However, it is interesting to note whether the company making the acquisition is paying for the target company with debt or stock. Generally if the acquiring company is paying for the acquisition with debt it may be a signal that the company feels its stock is cheap. Similarly a company that is on a rampage of acquisitions using its own stock may be a clear signal to investors that the managers of the corporation see their stock as being overvalued.

You can also make money by tracking when companies first start to pay dividends or miss a dividend payment. Not surprisingly, there seems to be a positive price reaction to the initiation of dividend payments and a negative price response to stocks which announced that they were eliminating dividend payments to shareholders. As you might expect if you have every held a stock that has announced a dividend cut the negative reaction to dividend cuts is substantially stronger than the positive reaction to dividend initiations. Despite this asymetry, significant returns can likely be generated by going long on firms that initiate a dividend program and shorting those which decide to cease dividend payments. The returns from this market neutral strategy seem to come predominately from the short side.

## All That Glitters Isn't Gold

To sum up, it appears you can make money by doing the following: First, avoid IPOs; don't buy the stocks for a period of three to four years after they become public. Unless you are a very large institutional investor, if you have an opportunity to buy the IPO at the offering price directly from the underwriter, you should probably pass up the opportunity. An exception to this would be the new type of IPOs that are run effectively as dutch auctions. When the IPO is run as a dutch auction, as opposed to its having a fixed offering price, you are much more likely not to be buying into broken IPOs.

You should look at secondary equity offerings in much the same way as an IPO. Generally, any equity issuance is a negative for a stock. By examining the aggregate amount of equity issuance relative to debt issuance, you can get a general idea of whether the market is frothy. Historically, when equity issuance spikes relative to debt issuance, it is an indication that the market may be headed for a cool-down period.

When it comes to share buybacks, pay particular attention to small-cap self-tender offers. If you see tender offers for small-cap stocks, buy the stock and ignore the tender. Share buybacks in the open market are also very positive signals. You should be able to beat the market over time by buying companies that have announced substantial share buybacks. While some people feel share buybacks are just a more tax efficient means of issuing dividends, it is more likely that the share buyback is signaling management's view of the company's shares effectively being undervalued.

All the instances discussed in this chapter reflect information asymmetry. The management of a company understands more about what is going on at the company than investors. If you take the actions of management as a means of signaling to investors what is going on in a company, you effectively want to be piggybacking on what management is doing.

Be like Groucho Marx: If a company is looking to sell shares to you, don't buy them; and if a company is looking to buy shares from you, don't sell them.

Instead, sell the stock of companies issuing stock, and buy the shares of companies looking to purchase shares on the open market. In terms of dividends, if a company eliminates its dividend, you should consider selling the stock.

# Chapter Seven

# Cash Is King

*Kicking Profits Down the Road*

IN THE OLD *POPEYE* CARTOONS THERE WAS A CHARACTER named Wimpy who had a catchphrase: "I will gladly pay you Tuesday for a hamburger today." You do not have to be some sort of management guru in order to understand that this is a decent deal for Wimpy, but not such a good idea for the restaurant.

Companies are better off taking cash today than relying on a buyer's promise to pay in the future. This idea that cash is king is behind a rather technical but very intriguing investment strategy called earnings accruals.

An earnings accrual investment strategy helps an investor try to outperform the market by effectively focusing on the quality of earnings.

## What's in Your Wallet?

In order to understand earnings accruals we have to first answer the almost existential question of what are profits? At the most basic level, profits are the difference between the sales a company generates and the cost of generating those sales. If you make a chair for $15 and sell it for $30, you generate a profit of $15. This is a pretty straightforward concept when the business is simple; however, real businesses are extraordinarily complex.

In a real business, cash expenditures and cash receipts are not nicely offset and spread out. Clients rarely pay up front with cash—often they simply sign contracts for goods or services to be delivered over a specified time period. The costs businesses incur in running their operations are never realized in nice quarterly payments; instead, inventory and factories are purchased in giant lump sums, which must be broken out into quarterly amounts and associated with the correct sales amounts based on accounting standards.

Accruals are effectively the part of earnings that are created by accounting standards. The other part of earnings comes from the cash that is generated through business activity. The earnings accrual investment strategy boils down to two fundamental points:

Point #1.  Trust cash earnings more than accounting earnings.

Point #2.  Most investors haven't figured out Point #1 yet.

Think back to the quote at the opening of this chapter. Earnings generated by customers like Wimpy from the *Popeye* cartoon result in anticipated future benefits being recorded as assets on a company's balance sheet. For instance, if the restaurant actually gave Wimpy a burger in anticipation of payment tomorrow, the company's books would record an increase in accounts receivable. Wimpy's promise to pay later is an anticipated future benefit. Accounting standards provide the guidelines that determine when future benefits can be recorded on the books. What the research seems to show is that earnings due to increases of assets on the balance sheet are uncertain, because they depend on accounting estimates of future benefits. If Wimpy doesn't show up tomorrow and pay his bill, then the company has to write down its accounts receivable and take a hit to earnings.

Say there are two restaurants: One has clients like Wimpy and the other has customers who pay in cash. The two restaurants sell the same goods and report the same earnings. The restaurant with customers like Wimpy can be thought of as having lower quality earnings. As an investor, if the stock prices of the two companies are the same, you should sell short the stock of the company that has customers like Wimpy and buy the stock of the company that has customers who are paying in cash. Why? Because the market is not delving deep enough into the accounting details to determine the quality of the earnings being reported. The market sees two identical restraints in selling the same goods and generating the same earnings. It doesn't realize that one of the restaurant's customers are all like Wimpy, and the other restaurant's customers are all paying with cash. At some point the restaurant with clients like Wimpy will see some of its customers not pay their bills, and its stock will fall. Effectively, when a business is generating earnings by accruals—or accounting—as opposed to cash activity, some of the anticipated benefits will not be realized and earnings will turn out to be overstated.

The earnings accrual story is that investors are too focused on the earnings per share numbers that companies generate on a quarterly basis without worrying enough about the quality of these earnings. Effectively, the market is overly focused on whether a company beat or missed quarterly earnings expectations.

Many investors don't dig deep enough into the actual quarterly reports to determine whether the earnings amount was due to cash receipts or accounting standards. The market only cares whether a company beat earnings—it doesn't care if it's because the company had cash-paying customers or clients like Wimpy.

## Show Me the Money

About 15 years ago research documented that investors tend to focus too heavily on corporate earnings in making buy and sell decisions about stocks. Academic research seemed to confirm what the deep value guys had been saying for years. Namely, that if you dig into the financial statements and actually look at where earnings are coming from, you can pick stocks that beat the market. It's the old Graham and Dodd idea—trust the cash flow.

What happened in the 1990s is that computerized databases provided a means to systematically test this idea using a large sample of stocks. What the research focuses on is an accrual measure of earnings that details the earnings that are generated by changes in current net operating assets.

Current net operating assets are technically defined as (Current Assets – Cash) – (Current Liabilities – Short-Term

Debt − Income Taxes Payable). Accruals are then the difference in net operating assets over a give year: Current Net Operating Assets (End of the Year) − Current Net Operating Assets (End of Previous Year). In practice, it is also common to scale the current net operating assets by the overall assets on the balance sheet. If the accrual number is increasing, then, effectively, earnings are being generated by increasing current net operating assets such as increasing inventory or accounts receivable. This likely seems complicated at first pass and for those who do not know their way around a balance sheet, it is simply easier to mutter to oneself, "High earnings accruals. That's bad."

The basic commonsense idea is that when accruals are increasing, the increase in earnings is deeply dependent on how the accountants are valuing current net assets, and over time the value assigned to current net assets is likely to be overstated. It is far more likely that Wimpy does not pay his bills and the accounts receivables on the balance sheet are too high, or that the inventory purchased loses its value, than that the opposite occurs. If net income is high because accruals are high, it is likely that the company will have to take earnings write-offs in the future. The data up to 1995 seem to back this belief up; investors tended not to sufficiently discount income when the income was due to increased accruals.

~

**The basic commonsense idea is that when accruals are increasing the increase in earnings is deeply dependent on how the accountants are valuing current net assets, and over time the value assigned to current net assets is likely to be overstated.**

What the data seem to show is that earnings due to accruals are not sustainable over longer periods of time. If we see high earnings today due to an increase in accruals, there's a good chance that these high earnings will not keep going. If, however, the high earnings are being driven by cash flows, the earnings are much more likely to stick around over longer periods of time. The real question for investors is whether the market realizes this fact. Do stock prices behave as if investors know that the firms with high earnings accruals are likely to experience large drops in earnings in the future?

Data collected by various studies over the last four decades shows that a hedged portfolio consisting of going long those stocks with low earnings accrual measure and shorting those stocks with a high earnings accrual measure generates a market neutral portfolio with the capability of generating a double-digit percentage rate of return on an annualized basis gross of transaction costs. Those stocks with a high degree of accruals or earnings due to changes in net operating assets tend to underperform over the next year, probably because the earning gains seem to be unsustainable.

The hedged strategy generates positive returns in 30 of the 38 years examined. This seems to indicate that the market does not know that earnings due to accruals are not sustainable and mistakenly pays up for them. Investors, it seems, are blinded by the actual reported earnings and oblivious to the quality of earnings.

The returns to the hedge strategy gradually declined after about 1998. Prior to 1996 the hedged returns are positive in all but one year. After 1996, however, only about half of the years have positive returns.

One potentially possible explanation is that the returns generated by the strategy are being arbitraged or traded away as investors seek to employ the accrual-based strategies. It seems that large sophisticated investors may not have understood about earnings quality prior to 1996, but once the papers regarding earnings accruals were widely distributed investors began implementing the strategies, and the pricing mistake investors were making of overpaying for low quality earnings was corrected in a few years.

This explanation seems possible but unlikely, given the fact that the majority of active equity investment decisions are still being made qualitatively, both now and in 1996. It is true, however, that many of the researchers who focused on earnings accruals were employed by large institutional asset managers, and that earnings accruals have been a favorite of many quantitative investors. In addition, the initial paper by Berkeley's Richard Sloan, detailing the accrual returns became one of the most highly cited accounting research papers in the country. Studies do however back up the idea of the accrual phenomenon being exploited, indicating that stocks with high institutional ownership exhibit prices that more accurately reflect the persistence of accruals, which would be consistent with the anomaly being exploited by liquid traders.

## Smoke and Mirrors

It also appears to be the case that firms with extremely high earnings accruals tend to have very illiquid and volatile stocks. So it might be the case that the earnings accruals trade is being exploited among the segments of the market where it is possible to actually trade. The small, illiquid securities might possess high earnings accruals but be almost impossible to short or buy without impacting the price.

What is surprising is that research indicates that the bonds of companies with high earnings accruals also tend to underperform over time. This is quite strange, because for the most part bond investors tend to be far more focused on cash flows than equity investors. An equity investor can price a stock based on nontangible future earnings growth, but a bond investor for the most part has to be focused beyond the reported earnings numbers, and he must examine debt coverage ratios where one would expect earnings quality to come into play with regard to investment decisions.

In any event, earnings accruals seem to work better in industries where working capital is a more important component of total assets. The industries that this strategy seems to work the best in are construction, toys, computers, and electrical equipment. The strategy does not seem to work very well among drug companies, mining companies, and energy companies. This makes intuitive sense, because an energy company's net working capital makes little contribution to the value of the company, which is instead driven primarily by energy reserves. For drug companies the key determinant of value is the lifecycle demand for the drug product—hot, approved, and nongeneric—not the degree of accounts receivables or inventories on the balance sheet. However, construction companies such as homebuilders have to maintain large amounts of inventory—recently built homes—on their balance sheet. If a home building company is growing earnings and at the same time massively increasing the unsold inventory, there is a chance the inventory may be overpriced. It does appear, however, that companies that are more responsive to earnings surprises tend to exhibit greater responsiveness to earnings accruals as well.

Earnings accruals seem to work relatively well as a means of avoiding companies likely to experience negative accounting events. Companies who fail to balance high earnings with accurate analysis of trends tend to overestimate their market demand and find themselves with excess inventory. This forces a restatement of earnings and the negative results that generally follow.

Avoiding stocks with a high degree of earnings accruals and buying stocks with a low degree of earnings accruals is a strategy that also appears to work globally, especially in those countries where the legal and financial systems bear some resemblance to those of the United States or the United Kingdom.

What is very interesting to investors implementing an earnings accrual-based investment strategy is that the timeliness of the data is not of paramount importance. With many of the investing strategies discussed in this book, it is important to get the data being acted upon as quickly as possible. With earnings accruals, examining data that has been in the public domain for several months does not seem to diminish the returns. The reason may be because the excess returns due to earnings accruals may occur around the time that a company being evaluated reports its next earnings report. Firms with high earnings accruals likely tend to report negative earnings surprises leading to the lower than normal returns—but these lower returns are realized around a negative earnings preannouncement or the actual earnings report.

It is possible also that the accrual-based excess returns are related to owning value stocks, as companies with high degrees of earnings accruals tend to be high growth firms. Still, excess returns due to earnings accrual-based selection criteria are much more persistent, at least prior to 1996, than excess returns due to valuation metrics. The excess returns due to earnings accruals can be adjusted for cash flow multiples traditionally used to select value stocks and the excess earnings accrual returns tend to persist.

One instance where earnings accruals were relatively helpful is the recent financial crisis of 2008. Prior to the crisis, banks reported growing profits primarily by issuing bad loans. These bad loans were capitalized on the balance sheet, resulting in high accruals and earnings. Thus the earnings of the banks were not due to higher cash flows, but rather due to accounting assumptions that resulted in higher earnings accruals. The banks basically issued bad loans and put assets on their books that were mispriced. As a result, earnings were unduly enhanced and the banks were substantially overvalued.

---

Prior to the crisis banks reported growing profits primarily by issuing bad loans. These bad loans were capitalized on the balance sheet, resulting in high accruals and earnings. Thus the earnings of the banks were not due to higher cash flows, but rather due to accounting assumptions that resulted in higher earnings accruals. The banks basically issued bad loans and put assets on their books that were mispriced. As a result, earnings were unduly enhanced and the banks were substantially overvalued.

---

## When the Bill Comes Due

An investor can make use of earnings accruals, but the strategy should probably be used in conjunction with other strategies. Researchers are now starting to make the case that the excess returns due to using earnings accruals started to disappear around 2000, or roughly four years following the strategy's initial discovery.

Investment strategies focusing on earnings accruals seem to be implemented more by hedge funds than mutual funds or other large institutional investors. In any case, remember that high earnings accruals resulting from an increase in balance sheet items like inventories and accounts receivable often mean that earnings are not sustainable.

Investors should also remember that earnings accruals tend to work better on the short side than the long side. For instance, it is better to avoid companies with a high degree of earnings accruals than it is to seek out companies with a low degree of earnings accruals. The reason is, of course, that the company with high earnings accruals may be obtaining earnings growth by overestimating the future benefit of accounting assets. A company with a relatively low degree of earnings accruals may simply be a cash-and-carry business. Stock screens based solely on low earnings accruals tend to highlight companies that are lower growth in nature and tend to run with positive cash flow. If a company has practically no accounts receivable and no inventory, it is likely going to have low earnings accruals.

Another negative with regard to earnings accruals is that, as pointed out earlier, many of the stocks that have a high degree of either low or high earnings accruals tend to be concentrated in small-cap, thinly traded securities.

The good news is that such securities are available to individual investors but unlikely to be traded by hedge funds or institutional investors. Thus, the anomaly is likely to persist among the smaller-cap stocks that are hard to hedge due to volatility.

Where earnings accruals can be very useful to the average investor is in guiding the type of fundamental analysis that should be performed. Investors should try to avoid companies whose current net operating assets are increasing—effectively avoid those companies that are exhibiting a high degree of earnings accruals. The reason is that earnings growth due to increase in balance sheet operating assets is not sustainable over time and is likely to be somewhat overstated.

In my mind, the best use of earnings accruals is to help you to find stocks to avoid. An investor should pay particular attention to companies for which inventories are rising relatively quickly. My experience has been that excessive rising inventory levels are an indication that the earnings generated from the inventory buildup are not sustainable. It also is likely that companies with a high degree of earnings accruals are more likely to report negative earnings surprises. You have to be careful, because earnings accruals will definitely increase when a company exhibits strong growth; thus it is important to use the earnings accruals in conjunction with other methods.

At the end of the day you want to find "Popeye" companies that are eating their spinach and getting stronger due to increasing economic opportunities. Similarly you want to avoid companies whose earnings are being driven by "Wimpy" customers. It is a bad idea to invest in companies that grow by selling hamburgers today when payment is not coming in until Tuesday. Find companies that grow earnings, not by increasing their net operating assets but by collecting cash. Ultimately, the companies' estimates of the value of their net operating assets tend in aggregate to be too bullish. For this reason, companies with high earnings accruals should be avoided.

~

**Find companies that grow earnings, not by increasing their net operating assets but by collecting cash. Ultimately, the companies' estimates of the value of their net operating assets tend in aggregate to be too bullish.**

# Chapter Eight

# It's Worth What?!

*Putting a Price on Value*

ONE OF THE BOTTOM LINE TRUTHS ABOUT INVESTING IN the equity markets is that you can't generate returns without bearing risk. If you want to make above average returns, you must bear above average risks.

A market anomaly is effectively an exception to the principle of no free lunch. With a market anomaly, you obtain extra returns *without* bearing extra risk.

There is a degree of consensus among researchers that, over long periods of time, by buying value stocks you can generate excess returns relative to the market. However, there is disagreement as to whether an investor who owns value stocks is bearing some extra amount of risk in exchange for the extra returns.

If you ask any business school professor what types of stocks you should buy, the answer is usually a powerful endorsement of value. This is not based on a shunning of exciting growth stocks or a miserly attitude. Rather it is a conclusion based on analysis of the data in both the United States and overseas.

If one looks back over the past 85 years, what you will find is that since 1927 value stocks outperformed growth stocks in 58 percent of the years. Several years even saw value outperforming growth stocks by more than 20 percent.

It is not uncommon to have people argue about the accuracy and relevancy of stock market data in a period during which investors were using slide rules to make calculations. Nevertheless, if you accept the databases as being sufficiently scrubbed and accurate, you come to the conclusion that buying those stocks that are considered inexpensive by various scaled price ratios has tended to generate excess returns over time. At the end of the day, value stocks, along with Tuesday's afternoon kid's meal at the IHOP, are one of the last free lunches left in the marketplace.

## Measuring Value 101

Many value studies work by sorting stocks into categories based on a measure of value. The stocks in the first group are relatively cheap while the stocks in the fifth group are generally expensive—all according to the measure of value. The metric used to create the groups is usually a price-to-book ratio, but it also can be the ubiquitous price-to-earnings ratio—stock price per share divided by earnings per share—or even cash flow multiples. I think the price to earnings ratio is a much better arbiter of value, but most studies show similar results regardless of what specific valuation metric is used.

The price-to-book ratio—stock price per share divided by shareholders' equity per share—looks at how much investors are paying as a multiple of book value. Book value is essentially the accounting value of a company. The best way to think about book value is as the difference between the accounting value of the assets of the company and the accounting value of the company's liabilities. Price is just what investors are paying for the firm's share price in the open market. The ratio can be thought of as an example how excited investors are about the company's future earnings prospects. A company in decline would trade at a low price-to-book value, while a company that is set to conquer the world would trade at a high price-to-book value.

———————————— ≈ ————————————

**The best way to think about book value is as the difference between the accounting value of the assets of the company and the accounting value of the company's liabilities.**

If you look closely at the data, you will see that the excess return attributed to value stocks is by no means stable over time. There are several years in which growth absolutely trounces value. One has only to recall the period of 1995 through 2000 to remember how growth can come into favor and stay there for a long time. Yet when a full multiple-decade period is examined, there is very clearly excess returns generated by value stocks.

In their 1934 classic *Security Analysis*, economist Benjamin Graham and his protégé David Dodd first put forward the hypothesis that value stocks have higher returns than growth stocks. Despite the popularity of portfolio management theory (PMT) in the last half of the twentieth century, statistical testing has confirmed the value anomaly using the price-to-book ratio as a value indicator or, alternatively, the P/E ratio.

Most investors, after examining the data, come to the conclusion that over long periods of time, value outperforms growth. The question as to whether value stocks are risk-ier to own depends on how you measure risk. Since becoming popular in the mid-1960s, the Capital Asset Pricing Model (CAPM), has become the paradigm used to evaluate the financial relationship between risk and return. This model basically boils down to saying if you want to make a high expected return you must bear higher risk. However, the risk that you bear is not related to the risks associated with any one stock. The reason is that by owning a whole bunch of stocks the risks associated with any one stock can be diversified away.

The CAPM determines the risk factor of each stock by forecasting its expected beta, or the degree with which the stock moves with the market. The thinking is that every stock faces risks that are unique to the individual stock. Will Apple's new iPhone be a success? Will China order a new plane from Boeing? Will Citigroup have to write off mortgage losses? These stocks' specific risks can have an effect on the stock price, but they are for the most part independent of each other.

If the risk of one stock is truly independent of the risks facing other stocks, the risk can be diversified by owning lots of stocks. If you owned 1,000 stocks each at an equal weight, any individual risk would be eliminated or diversified away. The only risk that would remain is the risk that all the stocks would move in a similar fashion.

For instance, in an economic slowdown fewer people would buy the new iPhone, China might cancel its plane order, and more mortgages would probably default. Even if you had thousands of stocks the risk of a recession could not be completely diversified away. Instead, there is risk that is common to all stocks. The CAPM sees this risk as the degree the stock will move in tandem with the market—the way you measure this risk is by seeing historically how the stock has co-moved with the market. This measurement is called a stock's beta.

Thus, the CAPM predicts that the excess expected returns, required by investors who hold stocks, are proportional to what is called the stock's beta, or the degree to which the stock will co-move with the market. However, empirical tests of the CAPM conducted in the late 1960s and early 1970s revealed patterns in stock returns that could not be described by the stock's beta.

One of the most prominent and persistent deviations from the return of a stock expected under the CAPM has to do with value stocks. Value stocks don't just outperform the market over time, they tend to outperform what you would expect the stocks to do based on their betas.

If you buy value stocks you seem to get a free lunch, an excess return that is greater than the risk you are bearing as given by a stock's beta. So either there is a free lunch, the risk measure is off, the data is bad, or you just got lucky owning value stocks over the last century.

## The Investor's Bias

One reason that value stocks may outperform over time is that people tend to be biased. Despite all the evidence to the contrary, people tend to believe in the hot hand.

Back in the day, someone could watch Michael Jordan sink basket after basket and conclude that Jordan is hot or on a roll. What this would mean is that Jordan has a greater chance of making future baskets. People are effectively wired to overemphasize the recent past, but statistical analysis of basketball players shows that a player's chance to sink a shot does not increase if he has come off a string of successful shots. Jordan may have looked hot, but the reality is that he was not. Jordan's chance of making a basket did not change if he made previous baskets. Effectively, Jordan's chance of making a basket was independent of whether he made baskets previously.

The data is very clear about this, but if you bring this to the attention of a highly knowledgeable basketball fan he or she will insist that players develop a hot hand. The way knowledgeable sports fans believe in the hot hand is the same way investors tend to believe in growth stocks.

Investors often give an inordinate amount of consideration to a stock's recent performance and its trend in sales and earnings. Like a basketball fan, it is possible that investors extrapolate growth from the recent past and incorrectly assume the growth will continue. While it is possible that a high growth company is truly growing at above average rates, it is also possible the growth company simply has had a few good quarters.

In reality, when dealing with earnings growth it is often the case that the omnipresent specter of competition and reversion to the mean rears its ugly head, and the historical growth rates quickly come back down to more reasonable levels. Ultimately, in aggregate it is possible that growth stocks never live up to their expectations set by the recent past. As a result, growth stocks tend to underperform expectations and lag the market. Thus, value's outperformance may in fact be due to growth's underperformance.

It is possible that investors irrationally project recent sales growth into the future and become overly optimistic

---

≈

**Investors irrationally project recent
sales growth into the future and
become overly optimistic about
firms that grew fast in the past.**

---

about firms that grew fast in the past and overly pessimistic about firms with lackluster performance.

Another possibility is that investors choose to invest in companies with strong fundamentals, whether or not the companies are fairly priced. That is, investors tend to overpay for growth because they like it, or maybe their clients' like it. No portfolio manager ever had to explain to an investment committee why they were holding Coca-Cola as a stock pick, but try explaining why you are holding Bank of America during the recent financial crisis. It is the companies that are close to distress and teetering on bankruptcy that a manager has some work justifying. Thus, it is possible that investors want to own good stable companies with growing earnings, whether or not those companies are fairly priced, in order to look good to clients. As a result, value outperforms growth over time, because investors irrationally buy growth.

Yet another explanation is that investors get caught up in the greater media and analyst coverage of growth stocks, become convinced that growth stocks are better investments, and overpay for them. The growth stocks are hyped by the sell-side analysts, and eventually investors start to believe the hype. Think of the dot-com mania played out not as intensely on an individual stock-by-stock level.

All the above explanations are psychological in nature. Value is said to outperform growth because investors keep making the same mistake over and over again, believing that this time the growth stocks will generate better returns—the explanation is that this is the way investors' brains are wired. While it's a nice story, ultimately when money is at stake people tend to be a little quicker with the uptake. It's highly unlikely that in aggregate investors would just continue to make the same mistake over and over again due to some weird cognitive bias. We are not talking about a hot hand in a Bulls game; we are talking about deploying billions of dollars incorrectly, time and time again.

## The Data Says . . .

One of the first economic explanations for the excess returns of value stocks is based on the idea that low price-to-book stocks—stocks with attractive valuation metrics—have a higher risk of corporate distress. That is, companies whose stocks are considered a value are much more likely to go bankrupt.

Using this logic, the value premium is the compensation required by investors for bearing the risk of bankruptcy, and the stock becoming worthless. Value stocks outperform over time because there is a greater chance that value stocks will go bankrupt. While many deep value stocks do in fact go bankrupt, the value stocks that actually return to good financial health increase in price and more than compensate investors for the losses on the bankrupt positions. The higher risk of bankruptcy for value stocks is eliminated when a diversified portfolio of value stocks is selected, but the risk scares enough investors away from value stocks so that they overpay for growth stocks (which on an individual level have a lesser chance of running into financial distress). If you dig into historical data, you find that low price-to-book ratios do in fact signal persistent poor earnings, while high price-to-book ratios signal strong future earnings. It is very possible that investors simply overpay for the cheery earnings of growth stocks. This seems to indicate that the excess returns of value stocks can be disentangled from the default risk.

One of the main challenges of researching value stocks is that the relevant rational and behavioral explanations are difficult to untangle. Every asset pricing test is a joint test of market rationality and the particular asset pricing model used to describe risk factors. In other words, whenever we observe abnormal returns, we cannot judge whether market participants behave irrationally or whether the model—and, hence, our understanding of risks priced by the market—is incorrect.

What we do know is that it pays to buy value, even if you measure value in a slightly different manner.

The Enterprise Multiple (EM) is a standard financial value indicator defined as the Enterprise Value (the value of common stock, preferred stock, and debt, minus cash) divided by operating income before depreciation (EBITDA). This is similar to the way an investment banker looks at valuations: The value of the entire company is determined by both its equity and its debt—divided by the cash flow that is due to the entire company. Such a measure is independent of the financing of the company.

If a company has a low EM, it is considered to be a value stock. Conversely, a company that rates a higher EM is almost always classified as a growth stock. It should be noted that the differences in average monthly returns between high and low EM ratings can be significant. Return differences are traditionally just under 1 percent for equally-weighted returns, but fall to about half a percent when value weighting is applied.

Over the last 45 years, the cheapest companies outperformed the most expensive companies by about 10 percent a year. As long as you are calculating value by taking the price and scaling it by a fundamental characteristic, it appears you can select stocks that will outperform over time. (Similar results hold for P/E multiples, whether we examine projected or historical earnings.)

## The Risk of Value Is Revealed

Not only does it make sense to buy value in the United States, but it also makes sense to buy value internationally.

With a few notable exceptions like Italy, value stocks outperform growth stocks in the vast majority of international markets. The difference may not be apparent to the casual observer, but on a price-to-book ratio, an international value portfolio outperforms an international growth portfolio by as much as 8 percent annually.

So if you are buying stocks in the United States or overseas, it makes sense to buy value. If you really delve into the data, you find that the excess returns due to buying value stocks are greatest during periods of recession. That is, value delivers returns when the economy is under pressure.

Effectively, the excess returns to owning value stocks vary countercyclically. Specifically, the excess returns increase during recessionary periods.

The international data along with the business cycle results are consistent with a risk-based explanation of the value premium, that is, investors become more concerned about potential bankruptcy in periods of recession and as a result flock to growth companies even more dramatically. Value stocks outperform because in recessions everyone becomes worried that the value stocks will go bankrupt. But the fears that lie in the heart of darkness are never realized, and when the economy recovers, the value stocks deliver strong returns.

This all could be due to government intervention. Essentially, the market does not price in the likelihood that the government, as the lender of last resort, will step in during a major recession and stop massive debt defaults from happening. The return from owning value stocks would look much different over the past 30 years if the Fed did not stabilize the market in 2008. It is very clear that government intervention is why a global recession has never, in fact, evolved into a depression. The risk to owning value is likely the risk a global depression actually materializes causing a large chunk of value stocks to default on their debt and go to zero.

If a company does not own debt—such as a large-cap technology company—it will never go bankrupt due to a recession. However, the same cannot be said of a company with a huge debt load. The price you pay to be able to go to sleep knowing that the companies you own will not go bankrupt in a depression may, in fact, be the basis of the value premium.

## Strength in Volatility

Studies have shown that the value anomaly persists not only over time but is influenced depending on the type of stock being examined. Some very interesting recent research shows that the value premium is higher for stocks that bounce around a lot in price. Highly volatile stocks tend to exhibit a greater value premium.

The reasoning here is that the more volatile a stock is, meaning the more its price tends to bounce around, the harder it is for institutional investors to hedge the stock with a short position, and the less likely an institutional investor will take advantage of the value anomaly in that stock.

Higher transaction costs and lower investor sophistication also appear to contribute to the excess returns on value stocks. That is, the excess returns generated from holding value stocks tends to be higher if the stocks being examined are primarily owned by individual investors.

One way to interpret these findings is as evidence that the value premium is caused by mispricing and that the mispricing is eliminated by institutional investors. The harder it is for institutional investors to engage in what are called arbitrage trades may be a key driver of the extent to which excess returns are generated by owning value stocks.

A similar logic indicates that if the value premium is caused by mispricing, it should be stronger for stocks with low institutional trading. Indeed, institutions are better informed than individual investors and on average should be able to scoop up mispriced value stocks more effectively.

## Shopping for Value Stocks

If you are going to buy value stocks, which value stocks should you buy? There are a few simple rules that can help you spot great stocks to buy:

1. **Buy value everywhere—in the United States and overseas.** The value premium is pervasive and there's no reason not to go global with value stocks.
2. **Time your buys to recessionary periods.** During a recession, investors become more concerned about bankruptcies and flock to growth stocks. This is a great time to buy.
3. **Look for stocks that bounce around a lot in price.** Other people might think these companies are headed for bankruptcy, and institutional investors will have a hard time hedging the stock with a short position.
4. **Buy stocks with higher transaction costs and low institutional ownership.** From a common-sense perspective you want to find value stocks that, for one reason or another, institutions have difficulty holding or are potentially uninterested in.

This of course points us towards smaller-cap value stocks as the way to go. Over long periods of time you will make excess returns and maybe, just maybe, not bear excess risk. Remember, you have to hold value stocks for long periods of time; value tends to outperform, but it is relatively difficult to know when value is going to outperform. If you buy value, you have to remain true to your discipline. Many a warning tale can be heard of the value manager who threw in the towel and switched to the high-glamour growth stocks just in time for the technology crash of 2000.

# Chapter Nine

# Earnings Surprises: The Gift that Keeps on Giving

~

## *How to Handle Earnings Announcements*

CORPORATIONS WHOSE STOCK IS PUBLICLY TRADED ARE required to report their earnings on a quarterly basis. One of the most interesting means of generating excess returns over the market has to do with focusing on what happens to a company's stock price after earnings are reported. The key question for the market is not whether earnings are strong or whether they have grown on a year-over-year basis, but rather how the earnings compare to what was expected by the market. When a company reports earnings that are substantially above or below what the market expects, it is called an earnings surprise.

At Zacks Investment Research, we created a metric that measures what the market's expectations are for corporate earnings. In the early 1980s, we invented the concept of the quarterly consensus earnings estimate. The consensus earnings estimate is an average of the quarterly earnings estimates issued by the sell-side analysts covering a given stock. The consensus earnings estimate is effectively a measure of what the market expects a company to earn on a per-share basis in the coming quarter. While the market's expectations for earnings may be unknown, the consensus earnings estimate is the only known proxy for these market expectations.

Extensive research over the past 30 years has shown that companies that report earnings better than consensus earnings estimates tend to outperform the market over the next several months. The reverse is true for companies that report earnings weaker than consensus earnings expectations; they tend to exhibit greater than market weakness over the next several months.

This phenomenon of the earnings surprise—as calculated on consensus earnings estimates—predicting excess market returns over the next few months is referred to in the research literature as post-earnings announcement drift. Post-earnings announcement drift continues to be extensively researched in the academic literature because it contradicts the belief that the market is efficient. It appears that by implementing a post-earnings announcement drift strategy, market-beating returns can be generated.

## The Financial Richter Scale

One way to generate excess returns over the market is by ranking stocks on the magnitude of their earnings surprises. Stocks near the top of the rankings—those that have reported large positive earnings surprises—should be purchased, while stocks at the bottom of the ranking—those that have reported large negative earnings surprises—should be avoided or shorted.

The resulting portfolio constructed from going long on the stocks of companies reporting positive earnings surprises and shorting the stocks of companies reporting negative earnings surprises is considered a market neutral portfolio.

The performance of a market-neutral portfolio is completely independent of movements in the market, and it is totally determined by whether the long portion of the portfolio outperforms the short portion of the portfolio. For instance, if the market falls 10 percent but the longs fall only 8 percent and the shorts fall 12 percent, the portfolio will generate a 4 percent return. Similarly, if the market rises 20 percent and the longs go up 22 percent and the shorts are up 18 percent, the portfolio still generates a 4 percent return. The return of a market-neutral portfolio is determined by the spread between the long side and the short side, not by the return of the market.

Various academic research over the past 30 years shows that market-neutral portfolios based on earnings surprises generate returns, gross of all transaction costs, of anywhere from 4 to 7 percent per quarter.

Before Zacks invented the quarterly consensus earnings forecast, earnings surprises were measured through a process called trend-line analysis. What this basically means is that, in the 1970s, earnings surprises were calculated as the percentage growth in earnings relative to the same quarter one year ago. The initial studies found that companies that reported strong earnings growth saw their stock prices rise over the year when the strong earnings occurred. However, something unexpected was found— the stock prices of the companies with the largest increase in earnings continued to rise faster than the market even after the stellar earnings were reported.

Stronger results are found when the earnings surprise is calculated based on the quarterly consensus earnings estimate. Over the past 30 years what has clearly been shown through extensive research is that companies in the top 10 percent of earnings surprises consistently out-perform the market over the next quarter, and companies in the bottom 10 percent of earnings surprises consis-tently underperform the market.

---

**. . . the stock prices of the companies with the largest increase in earnings continued to rise faster than the market even after the stellar earnings were reported.**

---

At the most basic level, after a company has announced earnings, if the company's earnings are substantially higher than analysts' expectations, then the company's stock should be added to an investor's portfolio and held for the next 3 to 12 months.

The post-earnings announcement drift has also been shown to be relatively stable across multiple time periods. Unlike several of the other strategies discussed in this book that tend to come and go in different periods, post-earnings announcement drift can be found across multiple time periods.

One study shows that the annual hedged returns between companies with extreme positive and extreme negative earnings surprise is positive in every year from 1988 to 2005.

While the studies may find differences in the magnitude of the market-neutral portfolio returns, almost every study finds that hedged portfolios created on post-earnings announcement drift do, in fact, generate positive returns. What is also very interesting about the studies is that across time periods the hedged returns are relatively similar. In the 1970s and early 1980s, studies showed the drift between 4.2 and 6.3 percent per quarter, and later data in the 1990s and 2000s show hedged returns of similar magnitude per quarter.

It also appears that earnings surprises tend to have predictive power over periods greater than the coming quarter. One recent study indicates the difference in returns between extreme positive and extreme negative earnings surprise portfolios following the earnings announcement is 14 percent over the next 12 months, 20 percent over the next two years, and 24 percent over the next three years. What is very clear is that by owning stocks that are experiencing positive earnings surprises on a statistical basis, you should outperform the market over the next quarter.

In addition, the post-earnings announcement drift does not appear to be very dependent on reacting immediately to the positive earnings surprises. It is important to remember that the post-earnings announcement drift is not the one-day pop that occurs due to the reporting of earnings—almost all of the studies discount this first day in measuring the price response to the earnings surprise. One study, which in all fairness is a little dated, indicates that roughly only 13 to 20 percent of the post-earnings announcement drift occurs in the first five days following the earnings surprise.

In fact, research seems to indicate that a good amount of the post-earnings announcement drift occurs around next quarter's earnings announcement. What this effectively means is that a positive earnings surprise this quarter tends to signal positive excess returns around next quarter's earnings announcement. It appears to some extent that positive surprises are predictive of future positive earnings surprises. This has led to the "cockroach effect." Ultimately, earnings surprises are a lot like cockroaches in a kitchen—once you see one you suspect that more are due to come out.

## Drift Away

The "cockroach effect" refers to the phenomenon that when a company reports one earnings surprise, it is likely that more earnings surprises will follow. You might only see one, but there are always many, many more. In the investing world, it is very similar.

Now if the cockroach effect were fully discounted by investors at the first sign of the positive earnings surprise, investors would bid up stock prices to reflect the fact that future earnings surprises are more likely to materialize. If the market were completely efficient, then earnings surprises would see their effectiveness eliminated—but that is not what the data show. Instead, we continue to see data pointing to the persistence of post-earnings announcement drift.

It is important when computing an earnings surprise that the earnings surprise calculated be apples to apples. This effectively means that definition of the earnings estimates and the earnings themselves must be using the same accounting procedures.

All the research into post-earnings announcement drift uses one of several definitions of earnings surprises. The earliest studies used a trend line extension model, explained earlier, where the expected earnings are the earnings of the company in the current quarter one year prior. More recent studies focus on reported earnings and consensus earnings estimates. The consensus earnings estimates are usually quarterly earnings estimates calculated by Zacks—as we have the longest history of consensus earnings estimates since we created the metric. Additional studies use earnings estimates made by individual analysts employed at a specific research or brokerage firm. Another means of calculating an earnings surprise focuses on the return of a company's stock price around the time of the earnings reported. The idea behind this price-only measure of an earnings surprise is that the price movement will incorporate all market expectations. Studies that compare different methodologies of calculating earnings surprises generally show that using the consensus earnings estimate is more effective than using the historical year-ago quarterly earnings. The consensus earnings estimate is about twice as effective on the long side and approximately 20 percent more effective on the short side as using the year-ago historical earnings as an estimate of market expectations. Additionally, the returns of hedged portfolios based on earnings surprises calculated from consensus earnings estimates are higher than the returns of hedged portfolios constructed from earnings surprise that are calculated based on last year's earnings.

Some investors believe that corporate earnings are extensively managed so as to decrease the power in the surprise data. These investors sometimes point towards companies like Apple whose proclivity is to keep earnings expectations of analysts low so they can always report a positive earnings surprise. These companies effectively try to underpromise and overdeliver on earnings results—much like a good manager tries to manage the people he reports to. However, research seems to indicate that sell-side analysts whose estimates are used in creating the consensus tend in aggregate to be too optimistic rather than too pessimistic.

So why does the post-earnings announcement drift phenomenon continue to persist three decades after being discovered? Why do earnings surprises remain such a powerful and consistent predictor of future price movement? As we have seen with several other investment strategies, the explanation for the existence of the excess returns is often as important in determining the validity of methodology as the return results.

There really are three classes of explanation as to why the earnings surprise phenomenon continues to persist. They range from rational or risk-based explanations to behavioral explanations, and explanations due to transaction or implementation costs.

## Risk-Based Explanations

The risk-based explanation of the excess returns generated by earnings surprises is that investors are bearing extra risk by holding companies that have reported large positive earnings surprises. The excess return over the market due to the large positive earnings surprise is simply a means of compensating investors for the increased risks. One possibility is that the effectiveness of post-earnings announcement drift may be correlated with macroeconomic factors. Some research seems to suggest that strong post-earnings announcement drift is largest following periods of high inflation. The research seems to focus on the fact that investors in aggregate tend to underreact to inflation much like a frog in a slowly boiling pot of water. If investors underreact to inflation, stocks with large positive earnings surprises that are being driven by inflation are not bid up enough as investors tend to discount the likelihood that inflation will persist. Consistent with this analysis, it has been shown that the returns of the hedge portfolio constructed using earnings surprises negatively predict growth in industrial production, real consumption, and growth in labor income over the next year.

Another potential risk-based explanation is that the post-earnings announcement drift is reflective of a firm's exposure to unexpected changes in liquidity. That is, firms with positive earnings surprises are more sensitive to fluctuations in marketwide liquidity than firms with negative earnings surprises. All these risk-based explanations suffer from one fundamental flaw.

Risk-based explanations are unable to explain how the risk exposure changes over time with the reporting of earnings. If the post-earnings announcement drift was really due to different risk exposure, that risk exposure would have to change with the announcement of earnings when the companies are sorted into their hedge portfolios. While there is some evidence that a portfolio of positive earnings surprise companies may have slightly different risk characteristics than a portfolio of negative earnings surprise companies, there is absolutely no indication that these risk characteristics or risk exposures vary over time with earnings announcements.

My basic belief, after working with earnings surprise data over a decade, is that for the most part stocks that report negative earnings surprises do have different risk characteristics than stocks that report positive earnings surprises, but the post-earnings announcement drift has more to do with how investors process data than with differences in risk levels.

## Behavioral Explanations

A more plausible explanation is that the post-earnings announcement drift is the result of the behavior of investors. One branch of this belief is that the drift is due to the behavior of individual investors. The basic idea here is that institutional ownership is negatively associated with post-earnings announcement drift. What this means is that post-earnings announcement drift is decreasing with levels of investor sophistication—the more sophisticated the investor base, the lower the post-earnings announcement drift. Additional studies have shown that higher media coverage regarding earnings surprises also tends to increase drift.

The basic thesis regarding this branch of behavioral explanation is that the post-earnings announcement drift is the result of investor overreaction to earnings surprises. The less sophisticated investors are, the more likely they are going to overreact to the earnings surprise. I do not buy this explanation, and instead feel that the roots of the post-earnings announcement drift lie within the way people process information.

Earnings reporting season is a literal tsunami of information. Most actively managed assets remain controlled by qualitative investment managers. A qualitative investment manager is someone who makes the decision to buy or sell a stock based upon whatever subjective information the portfolio manager is considering, but it is not a decision made overnight in reaction to an earnings report.

Think of the qualitative portfolio manager as the classic old-school manager who buys stock that he knows. These are the types of portfolio managers who like to talk to the management of the company before investing. Such managers cannot process the information contained in the hundreds of earnings reports in their potential investible universe. Earnings information that is contradictory to their established portfolio takes time to incorporate into their decision making process. These qualitative portfolio managers take some time to go from owning no shares in a security to holding a large percentage of their portfolio in a company they may not be very familiar with.

---

~

**Earnings reporting season is a literal tsunami of information. Most actively managed assets remain controlled by qualitative investment managers. A qualitative investment manager is someone who makes the decision to buy or sell a stock based upon whatever subjective information the portfolio manager is considering, but it is not a decision made overnight in reaction to an earnings report.**

---

Quite simply, it takes an individual or team of individuals some time to evaluate the earnings reports and make a decision to buy or sell a stock. Before putting millions, or, in some cases, tens or hundreds of millions of dollars to work in a stock, additional fundamental research must be conducted. The portfolio manager must become comfortable with the new earnings information; he must question the information and change conclusions he has previously held. As a result of the need to qualitatively evaluate purchase decisions, these institutional investment managers experience a delay in reacting to the earnings surprise.

Thus, the post-earnings announcement drift is not due to overreaction by unsophisticated players, but rather underreaction by large institutional managers. It takes a large investor significant time to evaluate the earnings and act upon them—this delay causes the post-earnings announcement drift. This explanation of the post-earnings announcement drift is backed up by studies that show that the returns of hedged portfolios constructed on earnings surprises are almost double when portfolio construction occurs during a busy earnings reporting period. Effectively, post-earnings announcement drift is stronger if the number of companies reporting earnings is greater.

## Implementation Explanation

Trading on earnings surprises is a strategy that involves a relatively high degree of turnover. Although some earnings-surprise-driven strategies do have very long holding periods, for the most part, strategies that consist of re-ranking stocks on a quarterly basis based on earnings surprises will involve substantial turnover.

One possibility is that the post-earnings announcement drift is not being traded away by institutions because of transaction costs. The basic idea here is that transaction costs hamper institutional investors from trading on the post-earnings drift. Backing up this idea, there does appear to be some evidence that the post-earnings announcement drift is higher among firms that are difficult for large institutional investors to hold.

One study focusing on the volatility of historical stock prices as a proxy for how hard a stock is to trade or short finds that post-earnings announcement drift is higher among stocks that exhibit high price volatility. Other studies have also shown that post-earnings announcement drift is higher for stocks that possess attributes that are likely to be associated with higher transaction costs.

Some studies show that the post-earnings announcement drift is reduced when adjusting for potential transaction costs, and others show the drift remains strong after adjusting for transaction costs. The data—like a switch hitter—goes both ways with certain studies indicating that transaction costs are grossly overestimated by researchers, while other studies indicating transaction costs are under-estimated.

Most studies, however, continue to show that even after adjusting for transaction costs, post-earnings announcement drift continues to exist. Thus, while transaction costs must by definition reduce the hedged portfolio returns of a post-earnings announcement drift strategy, the excess returns of the strategy will probably continue to persist even after adjusting for transaction costs.

## How to Work the Surprises

A study of institutional trading activity indicates that institutions actively use earnings surprises in their investment strategies. Post-earnings announcement drift is more likely to be implemented by institutions that are focused on short-term investments rather than those who are focused on the long term. It does appear that post-earnings announcement drift is not the predominant strategy used by institutions; instead institutions are more likely to focus on strategies such as price momentum.

Institutional traders also tend to implement a post-earnings announcement drift strategy less aggressively among companies that have higher transaction costs. One very interesting study shows that institutional trading 5 to 10 days prior to an earnings announcement tends not to generate excess returns, but trades immediately following earnings announcements tend to generate strong excess returns. This would be consistent with firms attempting to exploit the post-earnings announcement drift anomaly and quickly reacting to earnings information.

All the data clearly show that institutional investors are profiting to some degree from post-earnings announcement drift. If the institutions are profiting from the drift phenomenon, the question remains: Who in aggregate is selling stocks into a positive earnings surprise? The answer, unfortunately, seems to be individuals.

There is not a lot of research on how individual investors use earnings information, but the data that are available clearly show that individuals tend to make mistakes in processing and trading on earnings surprises. Studies have shown that stocks sold by individuals earn higher subsequent returns after being sold than stocks that are bought by individuals.

One study actually finds that individuals account for roughly 30 percent of all trading around earnings announcements. However, behavioral experiments conducted on individuals tend to show that they become more risk averse when dealing with gains and become risk seeking when dealing with losses. What this means is that when dealing with gains people lose their nerve to take risk, but when dealing with losses they want to take more risk. One only has to think of the gambler in Vegas who becomes more reckless with his betting as his losses mount. The reason is that the gambler wants to get even and starts making bigger and bigger bets to get there.

This behavioral bias could help explain the post-earnings announcement drift. Individuals will tend to be risk averse and likely to sell a winning position too soon. A company that reports a positive earnings surprise shoots up in value. The investors holding the position are likely dealing with large gains and as a result may become more risk averse, and in aggregate this bias could cause investors to sell the winning position too early. Thus, the stock of the company is seen over time as underreacting to the positive earnings surprise, and positive earnings announcement drift is observed.

Similarly, when dealing with losses, individuals tend to be risk-seeking. Risk-seeking investors would likely hold onto a losing position for too long. When dealing with losses, investors tend to gamble more, and the gambler is more willing to let a losing position ride in an attempt to get back to even. This would effectively cause a company's stock price to underreact to a negative earnings surprise. Such behavior is probably more prevalent with individuals than institutions, but is likely experienced to some degree by institutional portfolio managers as well.

In any case, when the post-earnings announcement drift is analyzed it remains relatively persistent and strong over time. As a general rule of thumb, investors can use the drift to their advantage by adding stocks to their portfolio that are experiencing large positive earnings surprises and removing stocks from the portfolio that experience negative earnings surprises. When a company reports earnings, if the reported earnings miss the consensus estimates it is generally a good idea to sell the position sooner rather than later. Similarly, when searching for companies to add to a portfolio, paying particular attention to companies that have recently beaten analysts' estimates makes a lot of sense.

In my experience the biggest risk to owning a high percentage of stocks that have recently experienced positive earnings surprises is that the portfolio tends to be slightly more volatile than the market. My basic intuition is that the beta of the portfolio might rise slightly relative to the historical five-year beta—but this increase is not of a huge magnitude. The excess returns generated by the post-earnings announcement drift from the positive earnings surprises more than compensate individuals for the risk from this slightly increased beta.

Chapter Ten

# A Time to Plant and a Time to Reap

~

*Seasonal Buying and Other Folklore*

As with most things in life, it appears there are seasons in the equity markets that are based on the calendar year and other factors. The markets ebb and they flow, and over the course of a half century, markets do appear to have some degree of predictability. However, it is unclear if the seasonality in the market can be used to help generate excess returns for investors. Nevertheless, there is some evidence that certain periods outperform other periods. To everything—including stock prices—it appears there is a season.

For instance, it looks like the market tends to rise more on Fridays than on Mondays. It also looks like small-cap stocks tend to outperform the broad market in January. Added to these concepts there is a whole slew of research that examines exactly when the market as a whole tends to perform slightly better. Is it the first trading day of the month? Is it the third term of a presidential four-year cycle? Does the market perform better in the 11 months following a January? Before we dig into the details of what is the best time to be invested in the stock market, we have to address the issue of data mining.

## Plowing the Ground

Data mining, or data snooping, is basically the problem of finding patterns that exist due to chance. With the increase in computing power and the wide dissemination of financial information, it is relatively easy to find patterns in the data that exist purely through chance and have very little predictive ability. For instance, if you examined stock data over the two decades from 1980 to 2000 you might come to the conclusion that stocks that begin with the letter M tend to outperform. The reason, of course, is that Microsoft was one of the best performing stocks over the period and it happens to start with the letter M, so stocks that begin with the letter M outperformed other stocks. A research paper might be written about the letter anomaly, but at the end of the day the strategy signifies nothing—it is simply a pattern that exists in the historical data that has very little chance of repeating.

Data mining is a major issue with seasonal trading strategies. If you examine the days of the week and the market's performance on each day, there must be one day when the market performs better and one day when the market performs relatively worse. It is unclear, unless there is a rational explanation, why the market would perform better on one given day of the week than another, whether this result is just the random distribution of return data or predictive of something in the future. With historical return patterns the key question is: Does the seasonal return pattern continue when it is examined with data outside the period initially used to find the pattern?

The other issue concerning seasonal data is that sometimes there is not enough data to have a meaningful or significant result. For instance, the research on which presidential party being in power results in better stock market performance is severely hampered by the fact that since 1945 there have been only 11 presidents. Any results saying this or that party is better for the market is hurt by the fact that the sample size is miniscule. As a result, it is often hard to conclude whether we are witnessing something real and predictive or just random distribution of historical data.

The best use, in my experience, of the seasonal data is to use seasonality to make minor adjustments to a base investment strategy. For instance, there appears to be a daily pattern whereby volume is slightly higher in the afternoon than the morning. This pattern makes some sense as institutions tend to trade in the afternoon and individuals tend to trade in the morning based on the previous night's news. As a result, the morning trading tends to be more volatile and have less depth. You don't alter your investment strategy based on this daily trend. Instead, when possible, you simply try to trade in the afternoon as opposed to on the open in the morning.

## When It Works

Investing using seasonal return patterns tends to work better with futures trading, where transaction costs are extremely low and leverage can be relatively high. I am adamant that timing the market is a losing proposition. In general, my belief is that the seasonal return patterns are more helpful at a cocktail hour than in an investment process. If you can remain invested in equities over long periods of time and ignore the volatility, you will be able to generate better returns for your portfolio than entering and exiting the market based on a seasonal pattern that may simply be the result of random fluctuations in return data. That said, the following seasonal patterns are ones that keep cropping up time and again in the returns of the equity markets, and they are worth further study:

**January Effect:** Small-cap stocks outperform large-cap stocks in the month of January.

**January Barometer:** How the market performs in January has some predictive ability on how the market will perform for the remaining months of the year.

**May/October Effect:** The market tends to be weak from May through October, and it's a good time to sell. Some refer to this as the May/Halloween Effect.

**Holiday Effect:** The market exhibits strength prior to the holidays when the market is closed.

**Rosh Hashanah Effect:** In the United States, selling on Rosh Hashanah and buying on Yom Kippur generates excess returns.

**Days-of-the-Week Effect:** Stock returns are higher on Fridays and lower on Mondays. The market seems to generate slightly better returns on Fridays and lower returns on Mondays.

**Congress Effect:** As amazing as it may be to those who watch CSPAN regularly, returns tend to be lower and volatility higher when the U.S. Congress is in session.

**Presidential Terms Effect:** In the United States, returns tend to be higher in the last two years of a President's term of office than during the first two years.

**Fixed Income Effect:** In the United States, bond returns are higher during Republican presidential administrations than Democratic administrations.

**Democratic Small-Caps Effect:** In the United States, small-caps tend to perform better in Democratic presidential administrations, while large-cap stocks tend to perform better in Republican administrations.

**Turn-of-the-Month Effect:** Historically there have been high returns for both large- and small-cap stocks around the turn of the month.

**Open Price versus Daily Trade Effect:** There is a strong negative auto-correlation between overnight return and intraday return. Most market return occurs after the market is closed.

**Weather Effect:** Sunshine seems to be somewhat correlated with stock returns. Greater sunshine tends to result in higher stock returns.

There is no broadly accepted explanation, but different times of the year seem to consistently have an effect upon the market. Personally, all my training and experience tells me that attempting to time the market based on seasonal issues is not a great idea; however, the return data seem to indicate that certain seasonal patterns have existed. Here are some of the more interesting calendar effects.

## January Effect

From 1926 until 1995 small-cap stocks tended to outperform large-cap stocks in January. In only 5 of the 70 years under consideration did small-cap stocks (the lowest 10 percent of stocks by market capitalization trading on the New York Stock Exchange) underperform large-cap stocks in January. From 1982 until 1995, small-cap stocks tended to outperform large-cap stocks on average by 4.5 percent in January.

These results are very significant from a statistical standpoint, and around 1995 it seemed that the January effect was a real phenomenon. Simply buy the smallest-cap stocks in January and outperform the larger-cap stocks by 4.5 percent in the month.

Not so. Over the next 15 years the January effect seemed to actually move to December. If you look at the difference between the Russell 2000 small-cap index and the S&P 500 large-cap index over the 15 years, you find that the spread is positive in December but actually negative in January. This is the spread an investor could actually implement cheaply using futures contracts, so it appears that over the past decade and a half the profit opportunity from the January effect seems to be dissipating. In a nutshell, this result illustrates the fundamental problem with seasonal investment strategies. It is very hard to determine if the historically observed results have predictive ability.

## January Barometer

If the returns for the market in January are positive, it's believed to be a signal that the rest of the year will generate positive returns for the market as well. Looking at the period from 1940 to 2010, we have a data set consisting of 71 years. We divide the returns into two numbers for each calendar year—the return in January and the return over the next 11 months.

In 44 of the 71 years the market was up in January. During those 44 years when the market's return in

January was positive, the remaining 11 months of the year generated a positive return 87 percent of the time.

In 27 of the 71 years the market's return was negative in January. When that happened, the rest of the year was positive only 52 percent of the time.

So what does this basically boil down to? Based on historical data over the past 71 years, if January is up there is roughly an 80 percent chance that the remaining 11 months will be positive. However, if January is negative, then the remaining 11 months of the year generate a positive return only about 50 percent of the time.

However, it appears that the majority of the failures of the January Barometer occurred relatively recently. Twelve of the 19 failures of the strategy have occurred in the 32 years since 1978.

You also have to remember that we are dealing with percentages. For instance, in 2010 the return in January was negative but the year saw a positive return for the market. The January barometer seems to have some predictive power, but the question is whether it can be used to help an investor generate excess returns.

The best market timing technique using the January barometer is to do the following: Invest in the market in January; if the returns are positive remain invested for the remainder of the year. If the returns in January are negative, invest in Treasury bills (a short-term obligation that is not interest-bearing) for the remainder of the year.

I do not recommend this strategy, as it is essentially market timing, and market timing strategies rarely work. However, from 1940 to 2006, annual buy-and-hold returns for the market were 11.9 percent. The strategy of buying in January and if the market return for January is negative going to Treasury bills generated returns of 12.8 percent annually in the same period.

The difference in return is not enough to justify implementing the market timing strategy, due to the fact that the January barometer can often give bad signals. Most investors would abandon the strategy after a bad year or two and thus would give up on the strategy after they are substantially trailing the market. The other criticism is that the return results are not out of sample. The January barometer surfaced in the 1970s, so a more accurate analysis would focus on returns since the barometer was widely publicized.

If the January barometer is applied to foreign countries, the results are somewhat mixed. A recent study examined whether the January barometer worked for more than 19 countries. The results are positive in the United States and Norway, but the strategy did not work well in the other countries, which included Japan, France, Spain, and Germany. This out-of-sample international test combined with the lack of a rational explanation makes me feel that the January barometer may be the result of data mining.

## May/October Effect

If you look at the returns of the stock market over every month, what you find is that the market is generally stronger in the November to February period and weaker in the May to October period. Additionally, many market crashes for whatever reason have occurred in October—most notably the big crash of 1929 and the 1987 collapse. The recent financial crisis began to worsen in September 2008. A commonsense strategy might then entail selling around May and buying back near the beginning of November. This idea is embodied by the phrase "Sell in May and Go Away."

Unlike the January barometer, research seems to indicate that the sell-in-May effect holds in a large number of countries. However, like many of the other seasonal-based strategies, it is very hard to find an explanation for the excess returns. Explanations vary from something akin to Seasonal Affective Disorder (SAD), to vacation timing, to a belief that investors are overly optimistic at the end of the year. What is strange about the international results of the May/October effect is that in countries in the Southern Hemisphere, such as Australia, the seasons are reversed. Explanations for the May/October effect regarding mood or vacation time don't seem to hold water since when it is winter in Chicago it is summer in Australia.

---

**Unlike the January barometer, research seems to indicate that the sell-in-May effect holds in a large number of countries. However, like many of the other seasonal-based strategies, it is very hard to find an explanation for the excess returns.**

---

Over the past 17 years if you were to sell the S&P 500 on May 1 and buy back the index on the sixth trading day before the end of October, you would have generated returns that were higher than simply buying and holding the index.

For whatever reason, generally speaking, stock returns in the winter seem to be higher than in the summer. It looks like, in roughly 65 percent of the years over the last two decades, the winter returns of the market have been higher than the summer returns. One way to use the May/October effect without engaging in market timing might be to go long on cyclical stocks in the winter and long on defensive sectors like the medical and consumer staple companies in the summer.

My basic feeling, though, is that without an explanation that makes any rational sense, we may just be witnessing some form of data mining. On the other hand, the view that there is some cycle of psychological optimism driving the sell in May phenomenon is not widely accepted by the markets, which might indicate that it will persist for some time.

## Holiday Effect

It appears to be the case that the market statistically tends to generate slightly higher returns on the trading day before a major holiday. The effect seems to hold for both small- and large-capitalization stocks. The results also appear to be statistically significant, and the strongest results tend to occur the day before the holiday begins. Labor Day and President's Day seem to have the highest pre-holiday level of returns. Again, this is an interesting result and may be useful to a futures trader, but it is hard to incorporate into an actual investment strategy. The reason is, of course, that there are only nine trading days a year when the markets are closed due to holidays. As an investor, the best advice you can glean from the holiday effects is to wait until after a holiday before selling.

It also does not seem to make any difference whether the holiday falls mid-week or at the end of the week. In almost all cases the pre-holiday returns are higher than average market returns for the day of the week that the pre-holiday occurs on. The explanation for this pattern is possibly that traders take the day before the holiday off and as a result there is a lack of sellers. Another possible explanation is general market optimism prior to a vacation day. We know from behavioral studies that the more optimistic people are, the more risk they tend to take, which would likely translate into more buying activity for stocks.

A related effect may be the observed weekend effect that market returns tend to be higher on Friday and lower on Monday. If you look internationally across 15 countries from 1997 until 2004, you find that the average Friday returns are positive in every country examined. However, most of these days-of-the-week studies have such high standard deviations that it is sometimes hard to call any result really statistically significant.

Most research seeking ways to profit from the difference in market returns on days of the week comes to the conclusion that it is very hard to profit from the anomalous behavior due to transaction costs and a high degree of volatility. Also, you have to realize that some day must by definition have higher historical returns, and another day must have lower historical average returns. Possibly it is simply random that the market tends to go higher on Fridays than on Mondays, and the result has no predictive ability.

From 1993 until 2010, the day before the President's Day holiday resulted in a positive daily return 82 percent of the time. Why President's Day? Why not—and that is one of the big problems with this type of analysis. At the end of the day the lack of a rational explanation for the seasonal patterns makes one cautious to actually implement any of them.

Under no circumstances can you bet the house that the market is going to rise on the day before Labor Day or President's Day, or any other holiday for that matter. The historical returns may just be a random distribution.

## Turn-of-the-Month Effect

One calendar anomaly that seems to be significant has to do with the first day of the month. Generally speaking the first trading day of a new month tends to be positive. This result is statistically significant and is often attributed to money flows. The basic idea is that market participants tend to put new money to work on the first day of a new month, and as a result institutional buying activity is higher than normal and prices must rise to clear the market. In addition, there is some data indicating that corporations tend to put off issuing bad news until the second half of the month, while good news is often issued at the beginning of the month. Finally, there is the fact that, in the United States and most other countries, paychecks are usually issued the day before the first day of the new month.

---

**One calendar anomaly that seems to be significant has to do the first day of the month. Generally speaking, the first trading day of a new month tends to be positive.**

---

This paycheck money likely finds its way into the stock market and helps boost returns at the beginning of the month. Not only does this happen with individuals, but it is also the way most pension funds and institutional corporate accounts work. Asset allocation decisions for pension funds are almost always made at month-end as opposed to mid-month. All this, as well as the strong statistical results, points toward the possibility that there is a real turn-of-the-month phenomenon.

Some investors have created market timing models that focus on being invested in the first day of each month and remaining in Treasury bills for the remaining days. Such models have shown historical returns about on par with buying and holding the index, but the proponents of such models argue that they are not invested the majority of the time. These tests generally do not take into account transaction costs or slippage from printed index prices. More important, though, is that the model does not work every year and it could still be the result of data mining.

## Political Effect

There are a few observed political effects in the U.S. market. When Congress is in session it appears that stock returns tend to be slightly lower and volatility higher than when Congress is not in session. Basically, annualized stock returns seem to be roughly 4 to 5 percent higher on the days when Congress is not in session when compared to the days when Congress is in session.

Some people have reasoned that the market performs better when Congress is not in session because regulatory risk is lower. Another possibility comes from polling data that suggests the congressional effect is driven by negative public opinion of Congress. Behavioral finance very clearly shows that investors who are sad tend to be more risk-averse, and nothing can make someone sadder than a session of Congress. Other political seasonal effects focus on how the market performs in various segments of a presidential term and how the market behaves under different political parties. For the most part, due to the lack of data and the question of the applicability of data going back more than two decades, the results need to be taken with a grain of salt.

Presidential investment cycle data make interesting fodder for the media, but ultimately have very little informative value. I fail to see the usefulness of trying to analyze the effect of political parties on the market going back farther than the Carter years. Quite simply, it is hard for me to believe that, if the market performed better when Dwight D. Eisenhower was president as opposed to when John F. Kennedy was president, it says anything about what will happen in the future if this or that party occupies the White House. However, if you ignore the question of whether what happened to the stock market during the last two years of the Taft presidency has any bearing on current market conditions, the data seem to indicate that the market performs better during the final two years of a presidential term.

## Shamanic Investing

For the cautious investor, I recommend first trying the two strongest calendar anomalies: Sell in May and Turn-of-the-Month. The Turn-of-the-Month Effect is statistically the most significant and also has the best explanation for its existence.

In any case, the usefulness of calendar trading strategies is limited in the equity markets. Futures traders could potentially make use of some of these calendar anomalies, but again the problems of data mining and statistical significance keep rearing their ugly heads.

⁓

**My belief is that by using some of the other anomalies in this book, active investment strategies can be developed that outperform the market over time—but engaging in behavior that borders on day trading because of what day is on the calendar is ill advised.**

If you engage in market timing using regular stocks, using these calendar anomalies is not advised. Over the years I have yet to find a successful investor who obtained his or her returns through market timing. My belief is that by using a combination of the other strategies in this book, active investment strategies can be developed that outperform the market over time—but engaging in behavior that borders on day trading because of what day is on the calendar is ill advised.

Chapter Eleven

# The More the Merrier

~

*The Use of
Multi-Factor Strategies*

BACK IN THE DAY, THERE WERE PINBALL MACHINES THAT after several good minutes of play would announce "multi-ball" and several steel balls would shoot from the machine. To the novice player the appearance of multiple balls would overwhelm his reflexes, but to the experienced pin-ball wizard, play would continue smoothly. In quantitative equity management the equivalent of multi-ball is a multi-factor model.

Multi-factor basically means that a model tries to combine different methods of generating excess returns into one composite model. For instance, we have seen that the stocks of companies that are trading at attractive valuation metrics tend to outperform the market over time. Additionally, we have found that stocks exhibiting strong price momentum also tend to outperform the market over the next quarter or two. A multi-factor model would try to combine these two factors and seek out stocks of companies that are trading at an attractive valuation metric as well as exhibiting strong price momentum. The idea here is that the combination of two or more factors will generate returns that are greater than by using any one of the factors singularly.

## Choosing Your Weapon

The challenge with developing multi-factor models is that the use of more than one factor can cause two potential problems. The first problem that can occur is a watering down of returns.

Say, hypothetically, that the valuation factor is real but the momentum factor is just an example of data mining—a relationship that has existed historically by chance and will not persist into the future. By creating a multi-factor model that makes use of both momentum and valuation, the valuation factor might be diluted.

Another serious problem that exists with multi-factor models is that they result in an investor selecting the factors that have the strongest recent historical returns. Often among those best performing factors are some that have done very well simply by chance. This causes real factors, those that have some economic basis for their existence, to be lessened by combining them with factors that exist purely by chance.

The other major problem with multi-factor models is that there is never a shortage of factors to select from. Even more problematic, there is never a shortage of factors that are performing well over the past year or two. Because of the raw possibilities, multi-factor models can be developed that seem to outperform the market historically. If in the development process a researcher is not careful, what eventually will happen is that the multi-factor model development simply becomes data mining on steroids. This leads to a fundamental problem in managing assets using a multi-factor model. When performance lags, which will happen at some point in time with any money management process, it is far too easy to switch out poor performing factors for factors that are performing well. This tendency may cause a manager to lack staying power, or good old-fashioned stubbornness, in his money management process. If you are constantly changing the philosophy on which your investment activity is based, you will always be switching during periods of relative underperformance, and as a result your performance will be far worse than by simply selecting a factor that makes some rational sense and sticking with the factor through good times and bad. Too often, investment managers employing a multi-factor model will essentially change the factors simply because the overall process is not performing. This factor rotation strategy, if not employed systematically, is the equivalent of using stop losses for an individual investor—you are always selling out at a loss, and it does not help overall performance.

***

**If you are constantly changing the philosophy on which your investment activity is based, you will always be switching during periods of relative underperformance, and as a result your performance will be far worse than simply selecting a factor that makes some rational sense and sticking with the factor through good times and bad.**

Many of the factors used in a multi-factor model relate to fundamental data. Strategies we have discussed previously such as post-earnings announcement drift, the accrual anomaly, valuation factors, momentum, signaling effects—all can be used as part of a multi-factor model.

However, there are additional multi-factor models that effectively focus on fundamental data. Fundamental data is information regarding a company's underlying actual business, and it usually can be found in one of the commercially available databases of stock information.

The fundamental data alone does not seem to rise to the level of generating excess returns, but when multiple pieces of fundamental data are combined the resulting metric appears to be greater than the individual components.

The two primary multi-factor methodologies that are well researched are the Piotroski F score that looks at statistics from nine fundamental metrics and the Mohanram G score that examines eight fundamental metrics. The F score focuses on selecting value stocks while the G score focuses on selecting growth stocks.

In a relatively efficient market, the fact that one company has a higher return on assets than another company would already be reflected in the stock prices of the two companies. The same could be said of almost any metric that is used in a fundamental scoring system. Any basic fundamental ratio that would be included in a multi-factor model would be widely known and also likely reflected in stock prices.

## A Whole Greater Than the Sum of Its Parts

The basic belief behind the effectiveness of multi-factor models is that the composite is greater than the components—the whole is greater than the sum of its parts. The idea is that the F or G scores accomplish what a good stock analyst does—identify stocks that can generate excess returns over the market.

---  ∼  ---

**The basic belief behind the effectiveness of the multi-factor models is that the composite is greater than the components—the whole is greater than the sum of its parts. The idea is that the F or G scores accomplish what a good stock analyst can do—identify stocks that can generate excess returns over the market.**

---

The biggest complaint against some of these multi-factor models is that their creation is a result of data mining. No one knows how many factors were considered before the scoring metrics were constructed and publicized. Also, only those models that seem to work get publicized.

A good example of data mining is the Dogs of the Dow strategy. This strategy focuses on buying the

10 stocks in the Dow Jones industrial average that have the highest dividend yield. The dividend yield is determined by simply dividing the expected dividend payment by a stock's price—the lower the stock price the higher the yield. The idea is that the dividend yield is a good proxy for value, and the Dow components with the highest yields are the Dow stocks that present the greatest value. The historical analysis of the strategy looked great. Unfortunately, if you performed the historical test not at year-end but instead at mid-year, the returns were not nearly as strong. There is no reason why the Dogs strategy should work if the portfolio is constructed at year-end but not at mid-year. Most likely the strategy was an example of data mining.

One of the easiest tests of data mining is to see if a strategy works in what is called out-of-sample data. This effectively means that you test whether the strategy continues to work on a time period or dataset that the strategy was not created on. One way to do this is to test the model on international data; another way is to test the model on a time period that is not considered in the construction of the model.

One of the first multi-factor models developed likely suffered from data mining. This early multi-factor model attempted to determine the probability of a company reporting a substantial increase in earnings in the coming year. The strategy showed hedged portfolio returns of roughly 12 percent per year by going long on those stocks the model indicated were likely to have an increase in earnings, and short on those companies the model determined were likely to report a decrease in earnings. However, when the same exact methodology was applied to another time period, the strategy did not work. Essentially, when the model was tested in a period that it was not constructed on, the model failed to deliver returns. The reason is that the model did not reflect any causal relationship and instead was just picking up on a statistical correlation.

## F Score

The Piotroski F score tries to help an investor identify value stocks that can outperform the market. Developed by Chicago accounting professor Joseph Piotroski, the scale rates companies according to specific criteria found in the financial statements. These criteria include profitability, leverage, liquidity, source of funds, and operating efficiency.

Basically, the F score looks for stocks with improving fundamentals. The belief is that value stocks with improving fundamentals are more likely to recover from their current depressed state.

The F score focuses on three broad measures of a firm's health—profitability, financial leverage, and operating efficiency. It wants to see these measures improving over time. It is also looking for profitability.

The score was developed around the year 2000 and tries to sort the value universe into buys and sells based on nine fundamental signals. Why nine factors? Why not ten or seven? Questions like these make me think that there may be some data mining at work. While the answer can never be known, it is possible that the results are stronger with nine signals, and perhaps 50 fundamental signals were tested but the nine best fundamental signals were used. Without extensive documentation of exactly how the score was constructed, the pernicious influence of data mining is always lurking.

Nevertheless, the F score focuses on items that can be gleaned from a quarterly balance sheet and income statement. Specifically, the F score examines: return on assets, the change in return on assets, cash flow from operations, an earnings accrual measure, change in gross margins, change in a firm's asset turnover ratio, change in debt ratios, change in the ratio of current assets to current liabilities, and whether a firm issued common equity in the previous year. All changes are looked at on a yearly basis—that is, the most recent quarter's data is examined relative to the same quarter's data one year ago.

The scoring system basically gives one point for each of the above items providing a positive value. If the return on assets is positive—give the stock a point. If the gross margin has increased from the year-ago quarter, you get another point. If the company has not issued any equity in the past year, you got it—you get another point. Thus, every stock in the value universe is ranked with a value from 0 to 9—depending on the number of points scored. Thus, there are relatively few value stocks that are given a ranking of 0 or 9.

Think of it this way: To be given a ranking of 9, a stock must score positively on every one of the nine items that are evaluated. This is rather unlikely, and as a result there are not many stocks with a ranking of nine.

A hedged portfolio is then created that is effectively long the 8 and 9 F-score-ranked stocks and short the 0 and 1 F-score-ranked stocks. Within the universe of value stocks, this hedged portfolio generates double-digit annual returns. The majority of this return comes from the long side of the hedge portfolio. The F score seems better at picking winners than avoiding losers.

Regression analysis shows the returns are not explained by other investment anomalies such as the momentum anomaly or earnings accruals. All is fine and well, until someone tries to update the returns.

Unfortunately, since it was discovered, the Piotroski F score did not generate similarly strong returns over the following 10 years as it did historically. Despite its lackluster performance since being popularized, the rationale behind the ranking is relatively sound—find the value stocks that are not complete junk that stand a chance of recovering their fundamental strength—and buy them.

Despite the reduction in returns when examined out-of-sample, the F score probably has some predictive ability. If you are searching for a means of selecting among value stocks, the Piotroski score is a reasonable approach, but its predictive ability seems to have faded. It is likely that the F score's effectiveness is not as strong as once believed.

The F score does not work as well when selecting among growth stocks—it seems to work better when the universe the score is run on consists exclusively of value stocks.

This may be because the scoring system essentially is a means of identifying those value stocks that are likely to recover from distress. Most value stocks are under some form of distress. Value stocks are cheap for a reason. As a general rule of thumb, investors don't like value firms' growth prospects. Some deep value stocks are in danger of defaulting on their debt.

The Piotroski F score tries to identify those stocks that are likely to recover fundamentally. Think of it this way: A value stock is a fighter who has been knocked to the canvas; the Piotroski F score is a means of identifying whether the fighter will be able to get to his feet.

The F score looks at fundamental items that an investor focuses on to determine if bankruptcy is around the corner. If the fundamental items examined are improving, perhaps the stock will be able to get off the canvas. Value stocks that tend to have a high F score are, like all value stocks, often under high distress, but the hope is that they are more likely to recover financially.

Like all true value investing, though, the portfolio held is by no means pretty, and it takes some real courage to buy and hold a portfolio consisting of such deep value names. Value investing is not for the weak of heart.

In addition, the components of the F score are all based on either quarterly data or changes in quarterly data over a year. For this reason the ranking methodology is not particularly time dependent—returns are not contingent upon reacting to data very quickly. At the end of the day, if you are employing the F score among value stocks in the worst case, it is simply randomly selecting from among value names, and it may in fact be providing some extra return kick by helping you avoid the value stocks headed for bankruptcy.

## G Score

Not to be outdone, Partha Mohanram, an Associate Professor of Finance at Columbia University, developed the G score to try to create a ranking methodology among growth stocks.

The rational explanation of the G score lies in exploiting inefficiencies related to growth stocks. In aggregate, growth investors tend to mistakenly assume that past sales or earnings growth will continue into the future. The G score tries to identify and avoid companies that, due to a lack of stability in historical sales and earnings growth, may be due to experience a growth hiccup. The G score also gives preference to profitable companies, as profitability tends to persist over time. Effectively, the G score looks for profitable companies with historically stable earnings growth—basically searching for companies for which future earnings growth bears some resemblance to the stable past. The G score also tries to find companies that are engaging in short-term money losing activities such as R&D expenditures that might cause earnings to be lower in the immediate term but may lead to greater long-term earnings growth. Additionally, if a growth company is spending large amounts of money on advertising or capital expenditures it may be an indication that quarterly earnings estimates can easily be met by simply reducing the spend. Effectively, the company may have at its disposal a cookie jar full of positive earnings surprises.

The G score looks at eight fundamental factors. Unlike the F score, the G score compares the value of these factors to industry median values. The industry median is simply the value for the economic sector that the company belongs to, such as software, hardware, or medical technology. For instance, in regard to Apple, the G score asks if the company's return on assets is greater than the return on assets of the other companies in the computer hardware business.

Basically, the G score looks for characteristics that investors traditionally associate with strong growth firms. In other words, the G score looks to eliminate those companies that are likely to fall off the track of high growth. It potentially works by avoiding losers as opposed to selecting winners.

---

❧

**Basically, the G score looks for characteristics that investors traditionally associate with strong growth firms. In other words, the G score looks to eliminate those companies that are likely to fall off the track of high growth. It potentially works by avoiding losers as opposed to selecting winners.**

---

The basic idea here is that growth firms whose metrics are better than the industry median are more likely to see their earnings growth continue. The advertising, R&D, and capital expenditure metrics all relate to whether a growth company is profitable enough that it can depress short-term earnings in exchange for long-term growth. For instance, R&D expenditure is carried on a company's balance sheet at cost, while the true value in terms of contribution to future earnings may be much greater.

The G score examines such factors as return on assets, cash flow from operations scaled by assets, the variance of the return on assets over the past five years, the variance of sales over the past five years, as well as R&D expenditures, capital expenditures and advertising expenses as well as a measure of whether the earnings growth is occurring through accounting accruals.

The G score is created by assigning a point for each of the separate cases where the fundamental value for a company is greater than its industry median. For instance, the G score examines whether cash flows scaled by assets are higher for Google than for other internet companies— if they are, Google is awarded a point.

Next, a hedged portfolio is constructed by going long those companies with a G score of eight and shorting those companies with a G score of zero. The findings are that the hedged portfolio generates excess returns, although most of the excess returns come from the short side. It appears that companies with low G scores tend to underperform your average growth stock more than the companies with the high G scores tend to outperform your average growth stock. Also, it appears that high G score stocks tend to experience greater positive earnings surprises in the future. This is consistent with the explanation that the G score identifies growth companies for which investors have underestimated future earnings growth.

The hedged returns resulting from the portfolios constructed by the G score look positive in most years, and are greater than what would be expected after controlling for the performance of some of the other strategies already discussed in this book.

The G score was popularized around 2005 and, sure enough, since then the returns have not been as strong. Much like the F score since its discovery, the G score has failed to live up to its historical returns.

## International Results and Distress

There has not been much extensive testing of the F and G scores in the international markets. A recent study investigated the F score in the Brazilian markets. Due possibly to limited liquidity in Brazilian equities and restrictions on short-selling, the results tend to show that the returns of the hedged portfolio created by the F score are actually stronger in Brazil than in the United States. Another study looking at the effectiveness of the F score in Japan also finds positive results.

A possible explanation for the results of the F score may have to do with default risk. If a company is likely to encounter some difficulty making its debt payments, one might think that the stock of the company should generate a higher rate of return. The argument is that firms likely to experience bankruptcy are riskier and investors should be compensated for bearing the higher amount of risk in holding these types of companies. However, the data seem to show the opposite. Firms that by multi-factor models are deemed unlikely to default on their debt or experience a credit downgrade actually outperform the market over time.

In fact, hedge portfolios constructed on measures of default risk generate positive returns. It appears that firms with higher estimated chances of bankruptcy actually earn lower returns. Stocks that fundamental metrics show as being safer—for instance because they have higher interest coverage ratios—look like they outperform over time.

This counterintuitive result is consistent with the market mispricing bankruptcy risk. By focusing on companies that are not likely to default on their debt, the F score potentially identifies companies that are mispriced or undervalued. Similarly, the G score may be identifying a mispricing of growth.

The G score gives a tilt towards stocks that are likely to continue to see strong earnings growth because these companies are investing in R&D and have shown historically stable earnings growth. The growth stocks with high G scores are less likely to falter because the quality of their earnings is stronger.

An investor must always be aware of the potential that both the G score and the F score are effectively the results of data mining. The scores seem to reflect something real, and it will be interesting to see how the two metrics perform over the next decade or so. In either case, use of the F score should be limited to value stocks and use of the G score should be focused on growth companies.

# Acknowledgments

⁓

I'D LIKE TO THANK MY EDITORS AT JOHN WILEY & Sons with a special thanks to Meg Freeborn and Kevin Commins. Both were a pleasure to work with and instrumental in helping make the book accessible to any reader. I was also very lucky to have such a talented production editor in Stacey Fischkelta.

Much of this book is based on the summary of the last 20 years of academic research which can be found in *The Handbook of Equity Investment Anomalies,* also available from Wiley.

Finally, thank you to my family—Laura, Sam, Rachael, and Maya—for providing me with all levels of insight throughout the years.

## A Special Thanks

I wish to acknowledge and thank the contributors to the *Handbook of Equity Market Anomalies* (John Wiley & Sons, 2011) whose summaries of the research in their specific areas of expertise were the foundation for *The Little Book of Stock Market Profits*.

Mitch Zacks